"I came to know Toranj through [...] detailing the life of her late daughter, Rowena. I was lucky enough to get to know Rowena through her loved ones, and the impact of her legacy has had a profound effect on me. From conversations with Rowena's friends, I learnt that her family was extremely important to her - and she held the opinions of her parents in the highest regard. 'Behind the Face' makes it easy to understand why. Toranj's story is one of incredible strength, resilience, and selflessness - always underpinned by love and loyalty. This book beautifully illustrates the mosaic of her life by exploring all the contrasting pieces of dark and light that are so important to the full picture. Thank you, Toranj, for a thought-provoking and deeply moving read."

— **Rose Knight**

"In this book Toranj allows the reader insight into her journey from wondering *why her life included so much suffering* and *why she was being punished*—to the realization that not everything is happening *to you* and into the knowing that things are always happening *for you*.

With this new awareness, along with the loving support of her cousin, she was able to move from bitter to joyful. Toranj then went on to develop a connection with her daughter—although no longer in physical form, Rowi is very much a part of her everyday life which includes 'out of the blue' magical surprises.

This is a powerful story of her awakening and transformation."

—**Dawn Smith**

"Behind the Face of Toranj Irani After suffering a traumatic loss, the book Behind the Face of Toranj Irani "is a heart wrenching story of a mother's triumphant journey from darkness to light. Her story will inspire you as she embarks on her path towards healing." Dr. Rhonda K. Lewis, Professor of Psychology, Wichita State University"

—Rhonda Lewis

BEHIND THE FACE

As for my baby girl, rest in peace until we meet again

TORANJ IRANI

PUBLISHERS OF O.G AUTHOR GENIUSES

Published by E&R Publishers New York, NY USA. An imprint of MillsiCo Publishing, USA
www.EandR.pub

This book is a memoir. It reflects the author's present recollections of experiences over time. Some names and characteristics have been changed, some events have been compressed, and some dialogue has been recreated.

Cover image by Dustee Self Photography. Permission granted.

ISBN: 9781945674648 (Hardcover)
ISBN: 9781945674655 (Paperback)
ISBN: 9781945674662 (Ebook)
ISBN: 9781945674679 (Audiobook)
Library of Congress Control Number: 2023900524

First edition

DEDICATION

To my late parents, Hootoxi and Tehmurasp, who raised me with love and dignity.

To Behram and Rooshad, in spite of facing torment suffering, and profound grief, thank you for believing I still had the strength and humanity to share my story.

As for my baby girl, rest in peace until we meet again.

TABLE OF CONTENTS

Foreword   8
Preface   10

Chapter 1 11
Chapter 2 16
Chapter 3 20
Chapter 4 23
Chapter 5 30
Chapter 6 34
Chapter 7 37
Chapter 8 40
Chapter 9 43
Chapter 10 51
Chapter 11 56
Chapter 12 60
Chapter 13 65
Chapter 14 74
Chapter 15 79
Chapter 16 84
Chapter 17 89
Chapter 18 96
Chapter 19 102
Chapter 20 108
Chapter 21 116
Chapter 22 120
Chapter 23 125
Chapter 24 130

Chapter 25 133
Chapter 26 137
Chapter 27 144
Chapter 28 148
Chapter 29 154
Chapter 30 160
Chapter 31 166
Chapter 32 176
Chapter 33 180
Chapter 34 192
Chapter 35 199
Chapter 36 208
Chapter 37 213
Chapter 38 217
Chapter 39 240
Epilogue 247

FOREWORD

"Life is ever unpredictable. Live your life to its fullest and view each day as a true blessing, as tomorrow is not promised. When you find those coins in your car unexpectedly, use them to be reminded of some of the best moments of your life."

Six years ago, Toranj would have never been the one to say this. Her journey has been far from easy, as many who read this book would agree. In hindsight, it appears that a culmination of life-changing moments and events, both big and small, is what has finally led to her own moments of awakening. This is essentially why we all have *chosen* this life experience, to be here at this time on the planet, as spiritual beings in physical form. But what did she awaken to?

She awakened from being that quirky timid girl to someone boldly speaking *her* truth. From the one who would suppress her intuition or compromise her dignity to please others to making her voice heard and standing up for herself. From feelings of powerlessness and hopelessness in the face of perceived authority to feeling empowered and believing in a larger purpose for her existence.

At the very end of the day, it is all about our belief in our own worthiness, isn't it? Her journey continues.

Behind the Face depicts how we tend to disguise our true feelings, thoughts, and emotions to conform to what we perceive as being acceptable within societal norms. We even call them sacrifices. But these sacrifices come from a deeper place, a place we are hesitant to admit exists—that part of us that lacks self-esteem and self-worth.

Her world came crashing down when the unthinkable became the inevitable. It was in these darkest moments when she summoned the courage to rise up and put her faith in divinity and in the ever-present spirit of her angelic daughter guiding her and lighting the way forward. You'll sense this courage in the pages of this book.

I strongly believe that life happens for you and not to you despite it being filled with moments that certainly do not feel that way. By recognizing this, the opportunity unfolds to wake up to your own power that lies within you. Your external reality can only reflect what your internal world perceives.

Uncovering the mystery of life after death, the unmistakable presence of loved ones, and stepping into moments of unquestionable trust and total peace is what Toranj has awakened to. The unshakable confidence and clarity that she has today would have been unimaginable once upon a time.

And for those who have lost a loved one – the synchronicities, the connection, and "out of the blue" experiences might provide the much-needed comfort, a sense of purpose, and a deeper knowing that unconditional love for you does exist on the other side. That is a reality you can believe in!

~ Danny R. Khursigara

Multiple Bestselling Author/TEDx Presenter/Transformation Leadership Expert/Co-Producer of *Soul of Success*

PREFACE

It hasn't been easy writing this book. My life has been a difficult journey, which I have buried inside me, hidden from the world. Outwardly, I am a quirky woman with a great sense of humor. Inwardly, I am very private—someone who has mostly kept my scars hidden despite having been humiliated, hurt, and emotionally abused.

As I pour out these words from the heart—and the hard reality of what my life has entailed—I remain diligent in the fact that this memoir is not written to take revenge on those who have caused pain to me and my family. I have released that burden to the Universe. Therefore, the Universe knows these characters' true identity, not by the names I have given them. But most importantly, I am Toranj. This is my story.

CHAPTER 1

As a child I was mischievous and carefree, a go with the flow type of girl. According to my parents, I always had something up my sleeve and ants in my pants. Unfortunately, my older sister Fara was never my partner in crime. She was the "perfect child" who loved to read Enid Blyton books and was a good student. Compare this to me, who loathed reading unless it was an Archie or Richie Rich comic digest. Our differences were always great but not greater than our love for each other.

I was born in Karachi, Pakistan to the most loving and beautiful Zoroastrian Parents, Hootoxi and Tehmurasp Khursigara. What is Zoroastrianism, you wonder?

Zoroastrianism is an ancient Persian religion that may have originated in 3500–4000 B.C. Prophet Zarathustra taught the importance of good thoughts, good words, and good deeds. These three very important values were embedded in us forever. Zoroastrian refugees escaped Muslim persecution in Iran by emigrating to India and Pakistan.

Zoroastrians are also known as Parsis in these areas.

My Dad came from a lower middle-class family. He lived with his parents and older brother. (Dad's brother is called Kaka in our Gujrati language.) They all lived in a one-bedroom apartment at 42 Parsi Colony. My grandfather worked for Lever Brothers but passed away of a sudden heart attack. Since my grandmother was a stay-at-home mom, Dad had to suppress his dreams to study architecture to support his family and took a job with Lucas Batteries.

My mom also came from a lower middle-class family. She lived with her parents and four sisters. (Mom's sisters are called Masi.) She joined Lucas Batteries a few years after my father as the secretary to Mr. Peter Pittman, the Managing Director from London, UK. According to Dad, he said when mom came for her first interview, she was holding grandfather's pinky finger for support.

Dad would say, "Mom came into my office and said 'Excuse me. I am Miss Hootoxi and I have come for an interview.'" Dad made us laugh with his impression of her meek and sweet voice. I don't know what happened and how she changed into a tyrant, but she did. Still, my sister and I would hysterically laugh at his silly joke, as Mom would throw something at him with a frown and smirky smile, including a mango seed one time.

My parents married on January 12th, 1961. In 1963, they were expecting their first child. Mom had no problems during her pregnancy and continued to work until her delivery, which came at the beginning of her eighth month. She had started to have contractions and sadly delivered a still-born baby girl. They were going to name her Sabrina. My parents were absolutely devastated and never knew what went wrong.

In 1965, Mom was expecting again. Her OBGYN, advised Mom to leave her job and take bed rest. She followed those orders and on June 22nd, 1966, my sister was born, a month before her due date. They named her Faranak, which means butterfly in the Persian language.

Instantly, Fara became the pride and joy of the whole family, especially on the paternal side. She was the first child, grand-child, and niece, until I was born two and a half years later, on December 5th, 1968, at 10 p.m.

Since Fara was running a fever at the time of my birth and wouldn't stay with anyone, Dad couldn't be in the hospital with Mom. The next morning before going to work Dad came to visit Mom and his second princess, so Mom thought. Mom was sitting in the hallway outside her room listening attentively to Dad's detailed account on Fara's fever and medication. After a while he looked at his watch and said, "Oh dear, I'm getting late for work."

Mom looked at Dad and said, "Aren't you forgetting some-thing?"

Puzzled by the question, Dad said, "No, what am I forgetting?"

"I didn't come to the hospital on a holiday."

Oh dear! "You didn't even remind me to see the baby."

Dad ran inside the room, immediately embracing me in his arms. Dad kept kissing my forehead. She often shared how she could see the wave of happiness in his eyes to have another daughter. Mom and Dad always wanted girls and their wish was fulfilled.

Then life began. It is Pakistani custom for family members to live together. But when my parents got married, my Rusy Kaka and grandma moved to another apartment because our house was so tiny.

Many years later I went to see the tiny house where I was born. It was also one bedroom and similar to most houses that people from my community lived in: a very small kitchen and one bedroom. Fara slept between my parents, and I had my baby crib all in that one room. The bathroom's walls and floor were made of concrete and not tiled. There was no hot water boiler either, so Mom boiled water on the stove and added hot water to the cold water to bathe us. There was no washer and dryer so everything, including our cotton nappies, were washed by hand.

Indeed, it was humble, but it was filled with love. During summertime, we were treated to ice cream and delighted in taking sips from my parent's favorite sweet drink, falooda.

These are cherished memories that have been told to me. I don't personally remember anything from my childhood house of 42 Parsi Colony, yet they all have an impact on me forevermore.

As time moved on, many different events happened, some small and others significant.

In 1970 Rusy Kaka asked my dad if he could keep my grandma with us. It wasn't that simple, that meant us having to move to another house.

According to my dad, Rusy Kaka was my grandma's apple of joy. When he fell in love with a widow—a Christian—it was unacceptable to my grandmother. This was the first time he'd ever really gone against her wishes. We became his solution.

By pulling a few strings we managed to find a new apartment complex called Jamshed Baugh. These apartments had three buildings with different layouts, ours being the largest of the three. Our new neighbors were Savak, Hillu Magol, and their children Cyrus and Villy.

Though our building was larger than the other two, it was still small. It had living/dining area, small kitchen, one bath-room, and two bedrooms. Since there were only two bedrooms, granny, Fara and I had to share a room. It was tight to fit three beds, a cupboard, a dresser, and a desk, and be okay with no privacy of our own. We tried not to dwell on this because we had no choice.

In 1975, Dad resigned from Lucas Batteries because his first boss, Mr. Pitman, returned to England and Dad couldn't see eye-to-eye with his new Muslim boss. Dad was honest to the core. His boss wanted to make money under the table and told Dad he could do the same—something unacceptable to him. So, after twenty-five years of loyal service to Lucas Batteries, Dad quit. I was six years of age at the time.

I still remember very clearly Mom temporarily had started working at the Austrian Embassy, but it was most certainly not enough. Our trips to our favorite restaurants and watching movies at Prince, Nishat, and Capri theatre decreased immensely. Eating chicken, meat, and our favorite Kraft cheese, which in those days used to come in a tin from UK was like a treat. We ate mostly fish, rice, and vegetables because they were much cheaper back then. But we were still happy and contented children. Although things and treats became less, their love and attention never lessened one bit.

Though our pockets were very tight we still managed to have family potluck dinner at our maternal grandparent's house with our Masi's and cousins Zarin, Dosi, and Dinshaw, plus continued to visit Dad's cousins Chum uncle and Roshan aunty and have fun with our cousins Cyrus and Danny. Family had always been important; however, they seemed extra special during those moments, a way to bring joy despite being poor.

CHAPTER 2

Karachi began as a modern, clean city. Horse racing and an active night life were its hallmarks. Hotels like Pearl Continental, Midway, Metropole, and Beach Luxury hotels would have daily cabarets and belly dancing. New Year's Eve was celebrated with open bars, dancing and performers would come from Iran, Lebanon, Turkey, and Russia to perform. Prestigious clubs like Sindh Club, Gymkhana, and Boat Club had facilities of bars, gambling, jam sessions, and a huge variety of cuisine to choose from.

That was Karachi then. It is not the Karachi I remember from 1973 on. Zulfiqar Ali Bhutto was the 9th Prime Minister of Pakistan from 1973 to 1977, a lawyer by profession and well educated from Berkeley University in California and the University of Oxford. He had amazing plans to make Pakistan a better country and it included building a casino to attract foreign currency to the country.

By March of 1977, violent protests were ignited by the opposition parties that did not want casinos and entertainment venues. It all ended abruptly when Pakistan became an Islamic state. To keep power, Bhutto stopped the growth of entertainment and forbade alcohol. In that moment, Pakistan changed from a modern country to an Islamic State.

Just around two weeks before Pakistan went crumbling with political riots, our parents took us for our very first trip out of Karachi. We visited Lahore, which is the second largest city in Pakistan with a lot of history to learn.

It was exciting to actually see the historical monuments about which we were learning in school: Lahore Fort, Badshahi Mosque, Minar -e- Pakistan, and Jehangir's Tomb. We also visited the twin cities, Rawalpindi and Islamabad. Then further up north, Murree Hills and Nathia Gali.

One memory remains vivid and funny about that vacation. Pakistan has two very famous dams, one of them being the Mangala dam. Dad had arranged with one of his military friends to show us the dam, as it was not open to public. For the entire drive there, Dad lectured us not to make a fuss at the army camp and eat whatever was served.

After being in the car, then the long boat ride learning about the dam, Fara and I were thirsty and starving. We were so ready to eat, even in the open shed with long wooden tables and benches with no cushioning. There was no cutlery and food was served on a plastic plate. We sat with the other army officers to eat. We were being watched by Dad like a hawk, making sure we were on our best behavior with appropriate manners.

When the food arrived, it was okras in gravy sauce with hot naan. Dad HATES OKRAS. As soon as Fara and I saw the okras we couldn't stop giggling. Dad kept on giving us glares to shut up, but we laughed even more.

Dad's friend Uncle Salman asked us to share the joke with him. Mom finally said, "Sunny has been lecturing the girls not to make a fuss and to eat whatever is served, but the truth is he hates okras. The girls find it too funny to see his red face. Salman uncle said with a laugh, "Sorry Sunny, that's all we have for today's lunch. You will just have to eat the okras without a fuss."

Poor Dad ate his lunch and hated every bite of it.

We teased him about this for years. This trip has such lovely memories as it was the only time the four of us had taken a holiday together.

* * *

Early morning of April 4th, 1979, Bhutto was hanged. I was in 4th grade. As the news broke, huge riots started all over the country. Schools were in lock down for many hours. At our school younger children were allowed to be with their older siblings in their classroom.

Scared, tired, and hungry, unknown to what was happening outside the walls of our school, we were all sitting quietly and only wished to return to our homes.

After Bhutto's death, Pakistan was never the same. Public buses and cars with innocent people were set on fire. Shops and houses were looted too. Many bombings had taken place in crowded markets. Pakistani people lived in fear not knowing what to expect. The country was under curfew for many months and schools didn't reopen until August of 1979.

When the schools closed in April, I was only ten years old. Not fully understanding the political turmoil and the disastrous situations in our country, all I knew was schools were closed that meant no homework, tests, final exams, and seeing some of the mean teachers. Since there would be no final exams all children were promoted to the next standard. For me that was truly a million-dollar lottery ticket, because I didn't care for the academics' part of school one bit. So, being young enough to not understand the full implications of the outer world, I embraced the gift I was given.

CHAPTER 3

My parents focused on our education and discipline quite a bit, but also wanted us to be kind, humble, and respectful. To achieve all these goals, they made sure we got into the best private school in Karachi, which was called Karachi Grammar School.

I am truly proud to be a Grammarian and grateful to my parents for sending Fara and I to such a prestigious school. Yet, I often have wished they would have chosen another school that was less expensive with friends of the same status as us.

School friends were fun, but when it came down to studies, I hated every moment of it. By fourth grade, my learning challenges became very apparent. Prior to that, my parents and teachers thought I was childish, only wishing to play and have fun. That was not the full story: I was never tested for ADHD and Dyslexia then, but I am a teacher now and can guarantee I suffered from both.

I rebelled against studies, which was my way to defend myself and hide what challenged me. To sit in a classroom of thirty children and listen to a teacher for sixty minutes was extremely difficult. Reading new and difficult words was hard. Whenever the teacher asked me to read or solve a problem or equation on the blackboard I either panicked or grew anxious. I tried my level best to read and solve the problem but because I was slow, my teacher would lose patience, she would ask me to stop, which made the other students laugh and ridicule me.

I vividly remember one such incident where my physics teacher asked me a question and I could only stand there, frozen and embarrassed because I did not know the answer. He got so irritated with me that he threw the white writing chalk on my face and asked me to get out of the classroom. I was around fifteen or sixteen at that time, but I sense the scars it left on my heart, ones that are only surfacing as I write these words.

What made it more difficult was Fara, who was clever and competitive, the daughter with excellent grades. Teachers loved her; however, two years later when they got me, they couldn't believe we were sisters. I was constantly reminded by my teachers what good a student she was and how proud my parents must have been of her. Most of my teachers made it sound as if it was the end of the world.

From primary class through high school, no teacher ever tried to understand that there could be some learning issues. How was shaming me in front of everyone going to help a child like me? Shame on those teachers, I still say. Being the opposite of them is what I try to do as a teacher today.

I believe children are different, unique, special, and beautiful. Each one has their own talents and personality, so why compare? There is no need to use harsh words like "you are dumb and lazy." Or, "You can't do anything right."

These harsh statements never leave your mind completely when you are the recipient of them. If anyone reading this book has a child who struggles through school always remember Maria Montessori's words:

"Everything you say to your child is absorbed, catalogued and remembered."

From the outside I was funny, cracking jokes and making people laugh. Internally, I was crashing. I felt embarrassed with myself, small and insignificant. As everyone congratulated Fara for her outstanding results they would ask me if I even passed the exam. I would give them a funny answer and laugh it off, pretending I didn't have a care in the world. That was not true, though, because I cared deeply.

I secretly cried and questioned God in my prayers: why was I different? As I grew older my questions evolved to things even more complex. What was I doing on Earth? Years ago, not understanding the reality of our purpose in life or knowing anything about spirituality, I secretly asked many unearthly questions to God. I never asked my parents or anyone else about what was on my mind during those times. It was such a challenge for me because I was too young to understand my thoughts and moods myself.

CHAPTER 4

In 1984 I fell in love with my hubby Behram. I knew B and his older brother since I was eight, as they were good friends with my cousins. B was a good-looking guy, twenty-three years old, six feet tall, a good physique, and thick curly hair with very sharp tanned Iranian features.

With our eight-year age difference my parents were concerned about the situation, just as I would be if I were them. However, I was young and in love. Like my family, B's family were also Zoroastrians, despite our families not knowing each other.

When we started dating, his older brother and younger sister had already left Karachi. His younger brother Carl was still in school. The first family member of B's that I met was his grandmother, Perin, whose name means "fairy" in the Persian language and is pronounced Pari.

The day we first met was funny and unforgettable.

She said (in Dari), "Behram, this is a boy." She was in shock and B couldn't stop laughing and assured her I was a girl. I had to show my earrings as proof.

She offered me tea and since we had just come from the beach, a hot cup of tea sounded excellent. She brought the teacups from the kitchen, I asked if I could have a spoon to stir my tea, Pari picked up a pen dipped it in my cup and stirred the tea. I looked at B in shock and he merely winked at me and nodded his head, indicating it was okay—just drink the tea. Over the years, whenever Perin asked for a cup of tea, I gave her a pen to stir it with. This was our sweet joke.

My parents were not happy with this relationship. The age was too big of a gap for them, and I was way too young to get into a serious relationship. They wanted me to study, enjoy, and explore the world and not get bounded at such a tender age. Second, his family had a lot of ongoing issues at their house. Zoroastrian community in Karachi was so small that everyone knew everything that was going on in other people's lives, either directly or indirectly.

B's family's life shattered when news spread about his dad having another woman in his life. Like any other woman would react, B's mom was devastated, hurt, and broken. Nearly eighteen years of marriage, when it all started, with four children made it more shocking for her life. She never would have expected it.

From what my parents had heard about the family they were very worried. People who knew them were warning my parents to keep me away. Though so many years had passed from his affair their house was filled with constant fighting and no love or stability. This didn't deter me—his parents' problems had nothing to do with B or me. Why was he being blamed for what his father did anyway?

At that time, I was too young to understand why B never invited me to his house. I met Pari many times at her own house, went to visit both his aunts, met his cousins, Carl would come with us on picnics and dinners but never his parents. STRANGE!

I chalked it up as just that and didn't pay any more attention to the matter.

After dating B for three years, Christmas of 1987 was the first time I was invited for dinner at their house and finally met his parents. My parents didn't want me to go by myself (in hopes of avoiding anything becoming official) so Fara and my very good friend Dinaz (D) came as my escorts.

We were greeted by several dogs at the entrance gate before we met any family members. Pari was waiting at the door of the living room to welcome us. Probably this was the first time she saw me in a dress and said to me with a big toothless smile, "Today you look like a pretty girl." And gave me a big hug.

B's mom came up to the entrance and gave us light hugs, B's dad remained seated on the couch watching TV, shook hands, but his concentration was still on his show. It was definitely not a warm welcome.

After our casual hellos, Fara, D, and I sat on the couch and tried to have a conversation with them in the midst of the loud TV. B's dad didn't take any part in the conversation, his mom kept running to the kitchen to check on food, and Carl had escaped to the neighbor's house.

When dinner was on the table, I noticed there was no table-cloth, placemats, just set of plates and forks dumped on the table with a few glasses that were half chipped.

Fara, D, and I didn't feel right sitting around while B's mom ran back and forth to the kitchen to bring out the food. We decided to help her and set the table, placing everything neatly upon it.

B's dad finally got up from his couch and came to the dining table. He came with the TV remote, but B grabbed it from his hands and shut the TV down.

I could tell his parents were socially awkward. They did not know how to play host. It was the most awful dinner I had ever been to. His parents barely made any conversation and when they did, their small talk was short lived.

B could tell my stress levels were high. He had been to my house many times for lunch and dinner, and he knew I was expecting the same from his family. He kept touching my knee, encouraging me that everything would be fine.

The only good that came out of this dinner was the delicious food. B's mom was definitely an awesome cook. She had made chicken curry and rice, potatoes, salad, and ice cream. After dinner she offered us tea, but we declined. I was ready to go home and put an end to that awkward dinner.

Upon my return back home, my parents asked how it had gone. I very unhappily said it was alright but didn't want to talk about it. As much as I didn't want to accept and admit my parents were right, I thought they maybe were. The next day B asked me why I was so quiet, but I changed the subject. After the Christmas dinner I didn't want to go back to their house. I kept thinking about how I could ever live with such people for the rest of my life. I was in a fog and a foul mood for days after that.

My parents kept asking what was wrong but I didn't want to share my feelings with them, or anyone for that matter. The only question that haunted me was what about B. Was I ready to break up with him just because of his crazy family? The truth was that I didn't want to lose him. The only way I came to terms with this turmoil was to justify that we'd have a separate house, not share one.

Being eighteen by this time, I didn't know or understand intuition. Looking back, I know it was whispering to me to walk away. And like a typical eighteen-year-old, I ignored it.

I continued on with the relationship. B was a good man, a bit overprotective and dominating, which is common in our country. He spoiled me with gifts, flowers, dinners to expensive places, and my every wish was his command. We had a wonderful time going for picnics with friends and having BBQ dinners on his roof top.

One day that spring, I was playing a basketball game with my friends. After the game was over and everyone left, very casually B said to me, "Let's get married."

I burst out laughing. "WHAT! Are you mad?" I thought he was joking and then changed the subject. Only he was not joking, and his face was quite serious.

"I am serious; let's get married next year." As he said this, I also became serious—and irritated—and replied, "What is up with you today? I am too young and still studying, what is the damn hurry?"

Without saying another word, B started his bike and left. He was going so fast on his bike that the residents grew angry because children were playing around, and he could have hurt somebody. My heart was pounding so hard I heard its every thump.

All my friends started asking what was that all about? I didn't reply and went home. I was full of emotions, as it was the first time I had ever seen B behave in such a manner. I refused dinner that evening and stayed in my room. Unfortunately, I didn't have a bedroom of my own where I could have gone to hide from others or cry my eyes out.

My granny and Fara were right in my face. That night I had the same anxiety attacks that I had after the Christmas dinner at their house. Again, I had the same nudge, that same voice telling me to walk away but I kept on brushing it off.

B didn't call that night or the next day. I thought he would, but he didn't and I was relieved. I needed that space and time. After two days, I pretended that everything was fine and went downstairs to meet up with friends. Still no phone from B.

Three days later I finally heard from him. He gave a sarcastic remark that if he wouldn't have called, I wouldn't have called either. To be honest I didn't know what to say at that point. I could still sense a bit of irritation in his voice.

I tossed the ball in his court and said, "You were the one who took off in a speed from here, I didn't."

Eventually things returned to normal between B and I. For more than a month he never brought the topic of marriage.

One day while B and I were eating at our favorite pizza place he casually said that his mom was asking about me. I asked why? B said he guessed it was because she hadn't seen me since the Christmas dinner.

A few days later, B said Pari had been asking about me too. Then he asked if I wanted to go to his house and meet with Pari and his mom.

The next day I went to meet my favorite person Pari, who was staying at B's house for a few days. I was most certainly happy to see her. She gave me a big kiss on my cheeks with a mouthful of raw tobacco.

B's mom heard our voice and came from the bedroom. I walked toward her and to show my respect, I embraced her with a hug. First, she asked how my parents were doing and then how my studies were coming along, and how many years I had until I was finished.

I thought, *where is this going?*

Then she said, "As you know, my father is in a nursing home, not keeping well with many health issues. Out of all the grand-children, my dad has always been fond of Behram. He will not live much longer and wants to see him get married. Then she poured out the words that I didn't want to hear: You and Behram should get married next year before he passes away.

Toranj Irani

For a few seconds I was speechless, and my heart was in my mouth. I just didn't know what to say. Instead of saying, "NO! I DON'T WANT TO GET MARRIED RIGHT NOW." All I said to her was my parents would never allow that to happen.

I wish I had the courage to speak the truth on how I felt, but I was too timid to say anything to her. Over the next four days, B asked me this question probably a hundred times. "Have you asked your parents?"

I thought I would go bananas.

I didn't pick up courage to say anything to Mom, but I took the opportunity to speak to Dad alone. Dad wasn't angry but very concerned. He kept asking what the hurry was. Then he asked me if I wanted to marry next year or if I was being forced. I told him the whole story of B's grandfather, but Dad didn't buy that.

Oh gosh! I'll never understand why I wasn't honest with my father and tell him that I was being pressured. I just could not bring myself to do it.

After a few days, Dad told Mom about it. Mom was extremely upset. She wanted me to finish my education, find a job, and mature a bit. However, I kept arguing for it, even though I knew deep down I didn't want marriage any more than I wanted to keep continuing on in my education.

29

CHAPTER 5

Band I got engaged on August 8, 1988, and married January 12, 1989. A day before the wedding we had some custom ritual ceremonies at our house. The house was hustling and bustling with family—a few from abroad—and friends. There was food and music and it was quite festive.

For my wedding I wore a white chiffon sari with silver shoes, small and beautiful diamond studs from my parents and Fara. I received four gold bangles and a diamond necklace from B.

I had gone to the salon to have my hair done but refused to have my nails painted or have professional make up done. When I was all dressed and ready to leave, my aunt SHE from London noticed my lack of makeup and lipstick and was not pleased. She ran to her makeup box and insisted I apply a bit for the pictures. I conceded, begrudgingly.

After the makeup was done, Mom started lecturing me about not walking like a boy and behaving like a girl, for that day at least. I rolled my eyes at her but followed the wishes that others had of me. Personally, the clothes and jewelry didn't work for me because I was still 100% a tomboy.

After the wedding was over and the priest was done imbibing his heavenly wisdom upon us, I realized I hadn't seen B's grandfather and asked where he was. B's face dropped and he didn't answer my question. I let it go for the moment but later I asked again. The response I got was nothing shy of an excuse. "Someone was supposed to pick him up from the nursing home but I don't know what happened."

My face went red with anger. I couldn't believe it. So, I went to B's mother to ask and she brushed me off. I wasn't upset because nana was not at our wedding, but I was troubled that the family had lied to me—to my entire family really. My fury came through in my wedding pictures, which definitely did not show a happy bride.

Our Zoroastrian weddings are a bit different. The couple doesn't leave until all the guests have left. Then the family members go with the couple to their new house, spend a few minutes there and then leave.

B and I had a new house, which was constructed on top of his parent's house: same address, separate entrance. So, we were together but at the same time had space of our own.

One day before our wedding I had intended to move some of my belongings into the home and that plan fell through because Roshan aunty had given a surprise bridal shower at her house. Since I had not gone to the house for a few days, I didn't realize that no one, including B, had made sure the house was clean and fresh.

When family members entered into the hallway and living room, you could easily tell it hadn't been cleaned in a while. B must have showered upstairs as his clothes and towel were still crumpled on the bed.

I was in tears, first the wedding and now this. My parents could see the irritation on my face and whispered in my ear that it could be fixed, that I shouldn't spoil my wedding day. But it was too late, too much damage had been done. I wasn't asking for a gift, which normally in our culture the husband gives to his wife on their first night together. All I wanted was a clean house.

My first night was not as romantic as I had anticipated either. I was exhausted and it was difficult to sleep. I fell asleep in the early morning hours and woke up about 7 AM. I had barely eaten the night before and wanted some tea and toast.

I went to the kitchen and opened the refrigerator, but it was empty. I thought, okay, since this is our very first day, we'll be eating breakfast with his family. I didn't want to go downstairs on my own, so I waited for B to wake up. When he woke up, we went downstairs only to learn that they had already eaten.

"ALREADY EATEN." Those words flew out of my mouth. Then the tears flowed, and B put his hands on my shoulders and said, "My family is not loving and caring like yours. You will have to adjust to certain things." Then he left for the market to get some basic groceries and cleaning supplies.

Whilst I was waiting there was a knock on the door.

B's brother Carl came with a laundry basket full of B's clothes. I asked if they were clean or dirty since they were all dumped and not folded. He said they were dirty, and his mom had said I could wash them, in the new washer.

UNBELIEVABLE!

After Carl left, I sat on the bed wondering if this was really happening to me. When B got home, I was still sitting on the bed with the huge laundry basket right in front of me.

He put his hands around me and said don't spoil your mood with these little things. You and I will take care of it together. He made tea, eggs with cheese and toast. I was starving and felt much better and less grumpy after I ate.

With a satisfied belly, we started cleaning the house, but little did I know that my dad was going to show up with Fara, Rusy Kaka's daughter Cheryl from Australia, Dosi, and the photographer with a video camera.

The video started right as they enter my lane. I am actually caught on tape dusting my windows. Instead of looking like a happy and glowing bride, my face and hands were covered in dust. When Dad saw B and I, he asked the camera man to turn off the video. He looked at me, then the laundry basket, then quietly but firmly told B that his daughter wasn't B's maid. He should find someone else to clean his house and do his laundry.

Thank you, Dad!

CHAPTER 6

About six months before our wedding, B's dad had an accident and was hit by a wooden crate on the seaport. His right thigh was swollen, and he was constantly in pain. He had to work in agony for a long time. It turned out that the hit wasn't his biggest problem. A while later he was diagnosed with Epithelioid sarcoma, a slow growing cancer that still made his health rapidly decline.

At this same time, my sister-in-law, who lived in the US, was also pregnant with her first child. B asked his mom if she still planned on going since his dad was not doing well.

Oh dear! B's mom started screaming and yelling. She asked him who he was that he dared suggest she not go to the US. Then she said that I could share some responsibilities of the house.

I was startled with that answer. B yelled back to her that I didn't marry her to take care of his family; especially a sick father who was not her responsibility.

The yelling and screaming grew louder and more intense and I just left and went upstairs to my house. My body was shaking, as this was the first time I had experienced such intense anger. Was this my life or a Pakistani drama?

Aunty did leave and as awful as she was things were about to get worse. My fathers-in-law's care fell on me and I had to do everything besides taking him to doctor's appointments, and the only reason I didn't have to do that was because I didn't drive.

Though I wasn't fond of B's dad whom I respectfully called uncle, I felt sorry for him. He was battling with cancer without the support of his wife and barely knew me, the person who was charged with his care. The situation wasn't great for any of us. His German Shepherd Iris was both of our saving graces on more than one occasion.

Life had taken a big 360 degree turn for me. From a free-spirited spunky tom boy, I had changed into a typical Pakistani wife taking care of everyone's needs.

B and I never quite had time to enjoy each other. His father's health and his mother leaving had taken a toll on our relationship. After marriage he was too busy working and when he got home, he was too tired to go out with friends or just spend quality time with me.

I hated my new life and desperately wanted to go back home. I had never seen such a disconnected family in my life; living together but yet not together. It was so bizarre to me and impossible to adjust to it all while remaining the person I was. The general message was do not complain, just comply. What I wouldn't have given for one of my dad's silly jokes at dinner or even Fara talking about her friends and studies.

I will never know what their life had been like before me, at least not fully. I only saw four children suffering at the hands of their parents. I realized how I'd taken my parents love for granted. I had been so lucky…up until now.

Something snapped inside of me and I decided to return home for a bit of time. My parents didn't ask me why and I didn't offer a reason. I just needed a break.

I remember very clearly for those two weeks that I was at my parent's house, B didn't once come to see me, or ask if I needed anything. I was very hurt but pretended that I didn't care. I freely played at a game detrimental to my wellbeing.

CHAPTER 7

After I finished my education, I had planned to start working but in September of 1989, I became pregnant with our first child. I was shocked, not that happy with the news, and felt ill prepared to be a mother.

At my first appointment with my OBGYN, Dr. Talati, the same doctor who delivered me twenty-one years earlier, asked my mom if I was doing okay? My mom asked why, and she noted that she'd been at my wedding and I looked healthy. I no longer did, and I had lost so much weight.

Mom didn't know what to say but assured her that everything was fine. A month later I was back to the OBGYN again, even a bit smaller. Now Dr. Talati was the best gynecologist I have ever known but, oh boy, she was a stickler. She was upset about the weight loss and apparent lack of self-care. I told her I was having a hard time eating and keeping down food. She admitted me into her maternity ward to try and get me back on track. I'd returned home after that but was admitted to the hospital several times throughout my pregnancy. It was that tough of a pregnancy on me, physically and emotionally.

June 2, 1990, at 6:02 a.m. I gave birth to a six pounds, two ounces, nineteen inches hairy baby boy. We named him Rooshad, meaning Pious Soul. At age twenty-one I became a mother, B was thirty.

Shad was the first grandchild for my parents and fourth for my in-laws. He was the first nephew for Fara and grandnephew for Thrity Masi, Katy Masi, and Khorsh Masi. After he was born, I remember asking my mom, "What do I do with him?" Mom chuckled and said to take care of him forever.

As much as I was not ready to be a mom, this beautiful baby brought me inner peace. All my attention was given to him, and I wasn't bothered with anyone else and gladly focused on my Shad.

Shad was truly a gift from heaven for us. We had lost three family members within four months before his birth, including paternal grandfather Jamshed, my favorite Uncle Ramie of a sudden heart attack, and my paternal grandma Ruttie. Shad's presence helped me to cope better and ward off my depression, which I struggled to manage.

* * *

That first Christmas in 1990, B and I had started to become a stronger family. He had gotten a tree and wanted to decorate it together. It was fun.

Even when B was tired after work, he would still make the effort to play with Shad or take us out for a drive. Most evenings I would put Shad in his stroller and take him for a long walk around the neighborhood or just meet with the other moms in the park. Twice or thrice in a week we would visit the neighbors across from our house, Maneck and his wife Bapsy. They had no children so for them Shad was a gift of joy.

What stands out most to me that first Christmas season was New Year's Eve. Our neighbors Martin and Fairy had invited all their friends to a New Year's Eve dinner to celebrate bringing 1991. My parents were going to a wedding and that meant that little Shad had to be left with his grandparents. Around 10 p.m., when the party was just getting into the swing of fun, Aunty came to the door and said that Shad was crying and wouldn't stay with them.

B and I left the party, only to see that he was sitting on the bed with uncle and playing. We didn't understand, even Uncle had a confused look as to why we were there early. B asked him if Shad was crying and before he could say anything Aunty said, "Shad was crying but now he is quiet." It was obvious that she was lying and just didn't want to watch him anymore.

B was very upset with his mom's behavior but not surprised. Whilst he was picking up Shad he angrily said, "You can be a nanny and a babysitter at your daughter's house, but you can't look after my son for a few hours."

This was an example of the impact family can have in your life. I had been so excited to go out for a dinner and have some adult time, but it came crashing within a few hours. After that I never asked Aunty to babysit Shad again. It was very evident to everyone, not just me, that her love only extended to her daughter's children. By her lack of love and affection for her other grandchildren, she missed out on the blessings of being a grandmother to eight amazing grandkids.

CHAPTER 8

August of 1991 Fara immigrated to Sydney to study at a reputable university and feeling quite ambitious. I was happy for her and sad for me—my best friend was leaving. No more endearing aunt, nephew bond with Shad, at least not one that was the same. Those are such precious memories, just as the thoughts of our conversations into the wee hours of the morning after Shad was asleep for the night.

Fara still jokes with me at times about how I used to call her all the way from Jamshed Baugh to Cyrus Colony and ask her to take me to Paradise Stores, which was five minutes from my house. Since I didn't drive or have a car of my own, whenever I needed something for Shad, I always requested her to take me. This drove her crazy—and she claims that is the very reason she moved to Australia.

With this closeness, Fara's absence from my life on a regular basis was noticeable. I felt the void and emptiness that was impossible to brush off. Sure, I had friends but not someone whom I could talk with an open heart.

May of 1993, I got pregnant again. It was an even more challenging pregnancy for me, filled with fear. I couldn't retain anything, not even water. At least once or twice a week I ended up in the hospital, sometimes staying there for at least two days.

Once again, I went to live with my parents, as there was no other option for taking care of Shad. Plus, my parents always made me feel better. By that time Shad was nearly three years old and going to a Montessori School. Since there were many other children who went to the same school, there was a van who came to pick them up. When Shad got home, Dad would come home for a few hours to feed Shad and then Mom would return from work and give him a shower.

Whilst being pregnant and unable to do much I did get to spend the best quality time I had ever spent with Shad. After he came home from school, we read books, colored pictures, played with blocks and puzzles. His favorite toy was his dinky car. He would have a dinky in one hand and a police car in the other. He would play around the corners of the bed; my big belly was his imaginary bridge. Shad was obsessed with police cars, police officers, and fire trucks. At that time, I had no idea that this was going to be his future.

In my second pregnancy, B desperately wanted a daughter. He had always addressed the baby as she. I jokingly asked what if SHE is a HE. He said that we'd just have to keep having children until we had a SHE. My answer was, "OH HELL TO THE NO."

I was having such a bad pregnancy and just the thought of having to deal with one more pregnancy gave me the chills. No matter what the gender of the baby, I was most certainly not going to have another child.

In December 1993, Fara came for her first visit from Australia. It was wonderful to have her back. When she left, Shad was only a year old but now he was a four-year-old who was a 100% boy who couldn't sit or keep quiet for a minute.

Fara and my cousin Mehernosh, who had recently moved to Karachi, were truly a Godsend for Shad and me. I enjoyed every bit of their company laughing and chatting but as soon as they savored their favorite fish, which was Bombay Ducks, I would run to the bedroom. That smell made me sick to my stomach! Still, I enjoyed every bit of pampering from my sissy and felt so broken when she left.

That December one last thing happened that created more work for me in the future, and that was B's dad having to get his leg amputated. I admired his courageous attitude and positive will power with it. He learned to do so much on his own, walk with crutches, shave, shower, and get dressed. He never complained about his pain, but occasionally he did mention the ghost pains he had where his leg used to be.

We all had stories playing out and each of us were impacted in different ways. My focus remained on making it through the last months of my pregnancy as healthily as I could.

CHAPTER 9

After spending nearly ten hours in labor, our sweet daughter Rowena was born February 18, 1994, at 8:05 a.m. at Lady Dufferin Maternity Hospital. This hospital was for women from all walks of life and out of respect for their privacy, men were not allowed in the hospital from 9:00 p.m. until 9 a.m. It allowed women time to walk around without their veils and protect their modesty.

Sweet Rowena was a bit darker skinned then Shad with red cheeks and jet-black curly hair. Her name was one I'd always loved, as it meant white spear or famous friend. In time, it proved to be a most appropriate name.

We called Rowena Rowi, and sometimes I called her Lola. Being born in the early morning I cherished everything about her and loved having her to myself before people could come visit. Mom felt the same way, as she could be with me.

When Mom called B and said, "It's a girl," he just couldn't believe it. Right at 9 a.m. he was at the hospital gate waiting anxiously to get in. He was ecstatic, happy with his son but surely on cloud nine to have a daughter. From the second he arrived, nothing mattered but Rowena. He just went straight to Rowi, embraced her, and kissed her sweet little face up.

"She is gorgeous," he said in awe.

I had to tease him a bit. I said, "No I don't think so.

She actually looks like a bird."

B frowned and told me to get lost.

After the delivery, Mom didn't stay with me at the hospital, but Katy Masi did. We laughed at the delightful nature of Rowi's true character. Whenever I tried to feed her when she wasn't hungry, she would turn her face away or place her tiny hands on her mouth. Katy Masi and I wondered how a newborn could even do that. However, when she was hungry and didn't get fed in a timely manner, she would howl so loud she woke up all the other babies.

* * *

After Rowi was born I stayed at my parent's house for two more weeks, before returning home to the chaotic life that existed there.

When Rowi was around four months of age, I started driving lessons and soon began to drive. With B gone all day, I didn't want to depend on anyone to take me to appointments at the pediatrician or anywhere I needed to go on errands.

I had to drop Shad off at school, take Uncle to his nursery, which B had purchased for Uncle after losing his leg. It was a wonderful opportunity for him to get out of the house and be independent. We had one car, which was used by all of us. B and Carl used their bikes but if I went anywhere, I had to keep in mind that I was responsible for dropping off and picking up Uncle from the nursery—and doing so on time.

I had developed postpartum depression after Rowi's birth, just like I had with Shad. It wasn't the babies as much as not feeling appreciated and like I was being taken for granted. It left me tired, irritated, and angry too often. I wasn't eating healthy food and taking care of myself.

Upon reflection today, I think what bothered me most during those times were the couples who enjoyed their married life and children, seemingly hassle free. Such pangs of jealousy existed within me. I was happy for them but doubting me. God often heard me ask, "WHY can't I have this kind of happy life? Why am I stuck with these people?" This was not the life I'd envisioned for myself and certainly hoped that it was not what God had in store for me either.

I was an absolute fool. It had taken me five years to see more clearly: B's mom wanted us to get married so she could have a free caregiver for her family, whilst she was enjoying life in the US with her daughter and grandchildren.

I felt like a robot, following commands with no choice. I didn't mind helping and giving a hand but there was absolutely no appreciation, kindness, or complimenting words; there were loads of complaints though. Uncle complained and mocked about everything including my driving and cooking. If I would forget something he would say that I didn't have brains. There were times when I wanted to lash out at him but instead, I remained quiet just because I knew that would cause tension in the house. But I knew one thing: I hated him and my life both.

B and my relationship was shaky, at best, but he did prove to be an excellent dad. His relationship with Rowi was unique, a pure soul connection, which was extremely special. It was written all over her sweet face: *I'm Daddy's little Princess.*

When Rowi was around six months old, she would only fall asleep with B. He would sit on the rocking chair, placing her on her tummy on his legs, and then pat her back. Most of the time, B would be asleep, and she would still be awake, but she would lie quietly on her tummy, making the cute gurgling baby sounds.

By age two, she knew exactly how to manipulate and get Shad in trouble. Every single day, she would be happily playing with Shad, but hearing B's bike, she would start crying. When B would enter the house, Rowi would be howling, pointing her little finger toward Shad. Every time I would argue that he had done nothing wrong, that they were just playing nicely with each other.

This went on for some time until one day B, switched off his bike at the end of the lane and quietly entered the house. It was a content house too, but when she saw B, she started howling and pointed her small finger toward Shad. From that day on, she was also known as "our drama queen."

Personality wise, Shad and Rowi were way different. Shad was mostly a good boy. He was a dare devil but at the same time obedient. He was extremely fond of my parents, especially Dad. On the weekends he would stay with them from Friday evening and reluctantly come home on Sunday night. Rowi on the other hand was always rebellious and head strong and until age seven would never stay at my parent's house at night.

* * *

After Zulfiqar Ali Bhutto was hanged in 1979, and Pakistan's great political unrest began, we all had to be more cautious. It led to uncertain times, where we were at risk of losing our livelihoods or even our lives. This has resulted in airlines and shipping companies not doing business with the country, as well. All this chaos impacted my dad, who worked at the shipping company Peroshaw Pestonjee. It left him discontent and he ended up opening up his own business in 1980: TIP TOP RENOVATION SERVICE. He became a contractor for house painting, plumbing, carpentry, and masonry. He enjoyed that job and was good at it. People loved the quality of his work.

After many years he finally got "the bad client," the one that people dread.

Whilst the work was being done, everyone was happy. After the project wrapped up, the son made excuses that the work was not satisfactory.

Dad was confident in his work and stood his ground, just as he knew that the son was making excuses for the money's worth. Dad knew the parents well and tried to sort things out with them, not their son. The father was quiet and didn't get involved but the mother and son both behaved very poorly with Dad. After a lot of arguments, the mother paid a bit more but not the full amount. Dad made sure laborers were paid but Dad never made any profit on that house. He also never hesitated to tell others how this family had cheated him with his money. He would never advise anyone to work for them.

This brings me to May 8, 1995, the day that completely changed my parent's lives and affected me profoundly. It was around 8:30 a.m. when I got a call from my parent's neighbor Hillu aunty. Hearing her voice, I knew something was awry. She asked me to get to my parents' house as soon as possible but would not tell me what was wrong.

Her fear made my own brain freeze as I tried to comprehend what I should do. I kept pacing from one room to the other, my hands and knees shaking with fear. What was I shaking about even? I had no idea.

B had already left for work; I was getting Shad ready for school. Well, the kids would just have to go with me. I ran downstairs and told Uncle there was an emergency at my parents, grabbed

47

the car keys, and left. I realized that Uncle wouldn't have any way to get to the nursery, but I didn't worry about that; I had to get to my parents.

All the way to my parent's house my knees and hands were shaking. Shad was asking why he wasn't going to school but to granny grandpa's house instead. He was excited to skip school to see his favorite people. Still, being five he sensed something was wrong but didn't know what any more than I did.

We pulled up and got out of the car. I began to run up the stairs, Rowi in one arm and Shad following behind me. By the time I got to the third flight of stairs where they lived, I was out of breath.

I noticed both the back doors that were opposite each other were open. As I was entering my parent's house, Savak uncle said, "Baby, come here" and pointed toward his living room across the hall.

Mom and Dad were sitting on the couch at Hillu aunty's house. They both were trembling. Hillu aunty had made some hot tea for them and was trying to feed them a few crackers.

I placed Rowi down, who began to cry. I didn't care. I wanted to know what happened to them! Most importantly, they were alive. I don't think I have ever hugged them so tightly before. I sat between them and asked what happened.

Mom didn't answer, she just got up to pick up Rowi, who was throwing a fit by that time. Shad had snuggled onto Dad's lap, and he finally said, "We got robbed."

Their account of that morning was horrifying. Dad had been packing Mom's lunch in the kitchen, which was very close to the back door. The back doorbell rang, and a man called out Dad's name. He opened the door, thinking it was one of his men. It wasn't. There were four men with guns there, scarves covering their faces.

Dad could only see their eyes. They pushed him aside and went straight into the bedroom. Mom was getting dressed, naturally confused about seeing four men with guns.

Too shaken up to continue telling me what happened, the harrowing account was turned over to Mom to finish.

She said they made Mom and Dad sit back-to-back on the bed with their hands tied to each other. The leader of the pack placed the gun on Dad's temple and said that if he didn't hand over all their money and jewelry, they would rape "your woman" in front of him.

Mom continued that Dad became extremely nervous, barely able to speak; however, she suddenly had plenty to say and told them to take whatever they could find, just so long as they didn't hurt them. And the robbers did but they were not satisfied. They demanded more.

All the while Mom kept asking who sent them over, enough so that one of the men got angry with her and asked her to be quiet. She wouldn't.

She said that out of eighty apartments, why did they end up at theirs? How did they know her husband's name?

Dad had told Mom to be quiet, but she didn't listen to the plea. One of the guys threatened to pull the trigger on Dad and that finally got her to be silent.

The robbers asked if they had anything in the safety deposit box, but before Dad could say there was, Mom said it had been sold off to educate their daughter in Australia.

My stomach was in knots as I listened to this story. I feared for my parents, just as I was grateful they were safe. No amount of money or jewelry were more valuable than their lives.

Then I went to see the house and the damage that these horrible men did. Roshan aunty and Danny came over and together, we walked through the house, which was an absolute disaster.

Clothes were strewn everywhere, the kitchen was tossed, and even the laundry basket was flipped over. They'd left no stone unturned, and it looked like a tornado had just swept through the entire home.

I was numb and overwhelmed as I stared sorrowfully at the destruction. Roshan aunty suggested to clean the kitchen first; however, I just lost it and crumbled on the floor and started to cry. My parents didn't deserve what happened and I wondered why God would let such a thing happen. It was another conflict with God that had me in a wreck—I was thankful to him that my parents were safe but distraught that he allowed such evil to happen to such good people.

Who could do such a thing? The only person that came to mind was the son of the parents who had not paid Dad the full amount. With our world the way it was we didn't bother to call the police, as they would have harassed my parents, nor did we tell anyone whom we suspected as we didn't have any proof. It's been twenty-seven years, since this horrible incident, which changed my parents' lives, especially Dad's.

Just in case the individuals who are responsible for the crime that was done ever read this book, here's a message for you: I assure you, that you will be punished someway, somehow for what you have done. Maybe not in this lifetime but in the next. No one gets away from the eyes of God.

After this tragedy my father was never quite the same. He started having nightmares and kept waking up, shouting in the middle of the night to Mom to see if she was okay. This affected his health to quite an extent.

CHAPTER 10

Nobody could have prepared me for how much my parent's robbery would impact them, and me as a result. In August 1995, Dad felt a sharp pain in his chest and jaws and then collapsed on the ground.

In Pakistan there is no 911 immediate help so the employees of Pakistan Cable, who Dad did some work for, put him in one of the office cars and took him to Liaquat National Hospital, where he could get some basic emergency medical help. Hospitals in Pakistan are unlike hospitals in other parts of the world: they will not proceed with any further treatment unless money is deposited up front.

Since Dad was not an employee of Pakistan Cables, none of the employees had any of his contact information. Luckily there was a Zoroastrian boy who didn't know me but knew my friend Natasha. She then called me to inform that he was in the hospital.

I rushed, delivering the kids to the neighbors (thank you Bapsy, Dosi, Dinoo, and Maneck) and making the important calls I had to make—especially to Mom.

By the time I arrived at the hospital, Mom and Roshan aunty were there filling out paperwork and depositing some money whilst Dad was fighting for his life.

We learned that he'd had a massive heart attack and that 70% of his heart was damaged. It meant that the next 72 hours would be critical.

I asked if I could go into the room to sit by him but I wasn't allowed to. I watched from the window and prayed to restore my strong dad from the vulnerable condition he was in. It was scary beyond belief.

The nurse saw me standing there tirelessly for more than an hour. She came outside and asked if he was my dad. "Yes," I said, "the best one anyone could..." I couldn't finish my sentence, choked by the tears streaming down my cheeks and staining my skin. Immense pain and sadness consumed me.

The nurse said he was in a lot of pain but sedated for comfort. She said that when he woke up in the morning, they would be sure to tell him that I was there for a long time, watching, waiting, and praying.

I stood there just couldn't leave, thinking what if I did, I might not see him alive again. He'd only just turned 65 and had so many things left to see in life. We needed him there to be a part of all those moments yet to come.

As friends and family heard the news about Dad, the hospital waiting room grew full. Everyone wanted to show their support by praying quietly, bringing tea and biscuits, or just helping in whatever manner they could.

I didn't want to leave Dad—or Mom—but had to because of the kids. The next day B stayed home with them, and I returned to the hospital for the day. Back at my spot by the window, looking from the outside in at Dad.

I hated seeing him like that and played movies in my mind of Dad being silly, witty, full of mischief, and driving Mom insane with his hysterical jokes.

We made it past 72 hours but Dad was still in rough shape. He was going to be in the ICU for a few more days. He wanted to see Shad, but it was against the rules.

I didn't mind being a rule breaker because this was Dad after all and if he needed Shad he'd see Shad.

Dad was calling Shad by his nickname "Bobby" from his bed.

During that evening's visiting hours B brought the kids to the hospital. There was a long hallway that led to the ICU. I told Shad we were going to run very fast down it, and he shouldn't let go of my hand or stop to ask me any questions. We were going to go inside Grandpa's room for just 10 seconds and then leave.

Poor Shad had to hear all kinds of instructions from me. With his hand in mine, we bolted down the hall and into Dad's room.

Thankfully, Dad's bed was right at the entrance, and he was awake. Like Curious George who always ran away from the man with the yellow hat, Shad got away from me and ran to his Grandpa. Dad opened his eyes, and to his amazement he saw his Bobby trying to climb on the bed.

Dad's face lit up like a Christmas tree. Even though he was attached to the monitors he still pulled Shad toward him and gave him his special teddy bear hug. He kept touching his cheeks and forehead.

I chuckled about how I had spent ten minutes lecturing him what not to do. It didn't matter now, and I could have cared less—the joy of Shad and Grandpa reunited was priceless.

Hearing the chaos, the nurse came around the corner. She was beyond shocked to see a child in the ICU sitting on the patient's bed, trying to ask a million questions in a minute.

The nurse was upset with me, and I got it, and did apologize. However, I also said that the only word Dad had spoken was his grandson's name. The nurse was not at all convinced with my story and asked me never to do that again.

The next morning when I went to see Dad in the ICU, he was looking so much better. He chuckled and said, "Rowi." I looked at him and said, "I see your witticism is back; that means you are fine."

We were only allowed five minutes and when I was about to leave, Dad said, "Tell the doctor to move me in a room by Saturday," I asked why and he said, "Saturday is Baywatch."

"DAD! You are in an ICU and you want to be moved to watch Baywatch. Absolutely NOT. I'm not saying anything to your doctor." He said fine but closed his eyes. A tantrum! That could be expected from Shad or Rowi but from my 65-year-old father, no way!

He even shared this desire with the cardiologist that evening, who busted out into laughter. Then he turned to Mom and said, "Mrs. Khursigara, your husband is not going anywhere. He is going to live for many more years. He will be shifted tomorrow to his own room so he can watch his favorite TV show."

* * *

Two weeks later, Dad was home. He had lost a lot of weight and was weak. He wasn't allowed to climb the stairwell to his third-floor house and had to be carried on a chair. Their apartment wouldn't work for them any longer.

Mom and I began searching for a ground floor house. All apartments in Jamshed Baugh were occupied. In Parsi Colony there was a vacant apartment but in a deplorable condition. Mom would have to spend a lot of money to make it livable.

In all the Zoroastrian communities where only Zoroastrian families can live, the new renter is responsible to fix it. When Mom, B, and I went to see the house I was in tears. Everything was in a mess. The concrete floors had cracked, windows were broken, and screens were torn, paint was chipping off the walls. The bathrooms had the old mosaic textures, which was just nasty. That was not uncommon in Pakistan; it would certainly be uncommon in the United States. With so few options that might work, that apartment became their next home.

After Dad's heart attack he wasn't allowed to work or drive; he had to change his diet to one with more fruits and vegetables. He ate everything that was given to him without a fuss, including okras. It was a small victory in the battle for his health. He was an easy patient and did everything that he was supposed to do, from taking his medicines on time to eating properly and regular walks. I admired his strength and positive attitude.

In December of 1995, Dad had bypass surgery at the OMI hospital. What are the odds; Chum uncle also had his surgery one day after Dad. Being cousins and good friends who did a lot together it became a joke that they chose to have surgeries together too. It worked out well though for visitors and family as well.

At visiting hours many visited Dad and Chum, and we could hear both the men laughing away with friends and family in their own room.

Fara came for Dad's surgery too, along with her then boyfriend (now husband), Dave. He was joyful to be around as everything was new and exciting to him, especially the rickshaws. He was a welcome source of laughter and kindness in a stressful time for us all.

Indeed, Fara's presence gave me so much joy and a bit of a break to help keep my sanity.

CHAPTER 11

1 996 was a busy year. My parents moved into their apartment, Shad started first grade, Rowi started at the Montessori school, and Fara was getting married to Dave in Australia.

We were all planning to attend her wedding, but money was extremely tight for all of us. Thrity masi was working for Qantas airlines so her ticket was free, but B and I were debating if I should go alone or just take Rowi—daddy's girl—with me. We figured that wouldn't work and went back and forth. Fara wanted us all there, so she ended up helping us with two tickets for the kids. It was a gesture that made a significant difference to us.

On December 5, 1996, my parents, Thrity masi, and the four of us flew into Singapore Changi Airport. Even after a year of Dad's surgery he was still very weak, we shortened our trip by taking a two-day break in Singapore, which was wonderful to see.

We stayed at the New Park Hotel, which was the central location for restaurants, shopping, and catching busses. We visited the Sentosa Islands, which took up a whole day for us.

The most fascinated and photographed place on the islands that make up the country is their Merlion. It is the national symbol of the city state of Singapore. It is depicted as a mythical creature with the head of a lion and the body of a fish. It looks beautiful at dusk with different colored lights and fountains.

Sentosa Islands also had water parks, a variety of restaurants, aquariums, dolphin shows, beautifully manicured gardens with exotic birds and flowers. Shad and Rowi were having a wonderful time chasing the birds, who flew away from them. There were also several night shows with dancing and acrobats.

Day two was more casual and at day's end we headed toward the airport just to learn there had been a big misunderstanding in the booking of our flights. Thrity masi and Rowi were booked on one flight via Jakarta to Sydney and the rest of us were on a direct flight from Singapore to Sydney. I knew there was no way that Rowi would do good for nine hours away from B and I. After a lot of hassles and arguments we finally got all seven of us on the same flight via Jakarta, which was already boarding. There was no time to even use the bathroom or call for a wheelchair. All of us—including Dad—had to take the seven-minute run to the gate.

Running for seven minutes doesn't sound too bad, but with luggage, a two-year-old in your hand, a six-year-old who bounced everywhere off the wall, and a weary father who was not given permission to walk fast, let alone run, it was not easy. We barely made it but we made it. A small victory for us.

We reached Sydney Kingsford Smith airport around 9:30 a.m., tired but intact. I was exhausted but super excited to see my Rusy kaka after eighteen years. Rusy Kaka, Cissy Kaki, and my cousins Gail, Julian, and Cheryl had migrated to Australia in 1974. Kaki and cousins had visited Karachi but not Kaka.

* * *

The next day Fara, her sister-in-law Megan, her friend Carolyn, and I went for our bridesmaid dresses. All three of us were wearing the same off shouldered long maroon dress with matching shoes.

Fara had a beautiful white lacey gown, with a long veil, mom was wearing a maroon ghara, which is an embroidered sari, Thrity was wearing her banarasi pink sari, and all boys were in their tuxes.

Fara and Dave got married at Chapel of The Scots on December 21, 1996. Rowi was a flower girl in a pretty white lacy dress. Her hair was slightly styled and had a beautiful hairband full of different pink and white flowers. She had six bangles in each hand and was holding a basket of flowers in her right hand.

Fara, Rowi, Shad, and Dad arrived at the church in one limousine. The ride was long enough that Rowi fell asleep in Dad's arms. When she woke up her hair was in a mess, her head band was crooked, and her expression grumpy.

When Shad met with her to walk down the aisle, he was such a good older brother, trying to hold his sleepy sister's hand and the rings. They walked in halfway through the church. All was well until...

Rowi saw her favorite person on earth—her daddy. She snatched her hand away from Shad, threw the flower basket on the floor, and ran down the church isle shouting, "Daddy," as if she had not seen him for days.

In a heartbeat, B picked up his baby girl. He tried to send her back to Shad but she clung to him like a little monkey. She was done for the day with the flowers and headbands. Poor Shad had to walk the remainder of the way alone.

*   *   *

Fara knew that I didn't drink alcohol—ever—but I took the champagne Dave offered me that day. When she had a moment, she leaned in and whispered, "What did you do with the drink?" I whispered that I'd watered the grass with it. The two of us chuckled at our little secret. Dave, on the other hand, had whispered to Fara that I could sure handle my champagne, which was amusing.

What stands out to me most about this wonderful day was that it was the first time in a very long time that I got to enjoy myself. I was truly on a holiday, on my own time and agenda. B was stress free, as well, and that was great for us to really enjoy time with each other. We visited Sydney Opera House, Harbor Bridge, Darling Harbor, Taronga Zoo, Blue Mountains, Bondi, Palm, and Manly Beaches.

Six weeks passed us by so quickly. And with our departure, it was also the last time I would ever see Rusy Kaka and Cissy Kaki.

CHAPTER 12

Relaxed vacation days cannot last forever. It was time to return to the complaints of life as I mostly knew it. I absolutely hated going back to that house and taking care of the no gratitude Uncle. Technically he wasn't my responsibility to begin with. But the call to do what was right as respectfully as possible was strong within me. I was taking care of him more than my own father.

Uncle loved to bicker and complain constantly and seemed to do that as much as he breathed. The food was always bland or too salty, the tea tasted like water, you name it, he complained. I even drove ridiculous, according to Uncle. How is that even possible?

In Karachi we had a lot of power and water shortages. Mostly all households had to call in water tanker to fill our house tanks. When the tanker came in we have to switch on the water pump to fill it up but one day I forgot to switch off the pump. He yelled at me saying I was stupid and didn't have any brains.

By then I had just enough of his bullshit. I turned around and said very politely, "You are absolutely 100% correct. If I had the brains, I wouldn't have married your son and stayed away from this family, but since I don't have the brains, I am stuck with you all."

His eyes were big and surprised. He didn't expect this answer from me. But by then I was just done with him and his whole family. I didn't want to be disrespectful but they all had tested my patience and I'd had enough.

* * *

In 1997, B's brother Carl received his immigration visa for the US. He worked in US for a few months and returned to Karachi in July to marry a girl he'd recently met, Naz.

I viewed this marriage as an impulsive decision on both parents ends. It was an arranged/love marriage, with Naz being only twenty-two, still in college, and without a job.

Naz was a very quiet and timid girl. Her parents were divorced when she was only three. The only family she ever knew was her maternal grandmother and uncle. She never really got to know her dad or his side of the family.

For Naz, Uncle became like a father figure, and she called him Papa. She gained a family through that marriage, which included Papa, an older brother-in-law, a nephew, niece, and a sister-in-law, which was me who drove her crazy but in a loving way. Yet it was so exciting for her.

She loved Shad and Rowi as her own children and they also became very attached to her. In fact, whenever they both were in trouble they ran downstairs for safety. Naz and I bonded extremely well. She was eight years younger, I treated her not as my sister-in-law but as my younger sister.

Since Carl didn't have any job and Naz was still in school they were always obligated for money. She had no say in that house, she didn't have access to TV, she didn't know how to drive. Carl couldn't take her for a honeymoon or even to a fancy restaurant. All she did was cook and clean for everyone but never once complained. She was happy to have a new family and desperately wanted to please everyone.

When Carl came back from US, things changed drastically for us again. Karachi was in another round of violence therefore the nursery business was slow. Since there were two additions in the family, I wasn't sending food for Uncle, they were doing their own groceries and cooking.

It was Carl's house and he could live there as long as he wanted to, but to be unemployed and not even attempt to find a job or help out at the nursery was making life difficult for everyone.

One day, B had a very stressful look on his face and he had all the utility bills in his hand. I asked him what was going on. B said Papa had given him the bills to pay, as he didn't have the money. I would have understood if some of the bills were given to us and a few Uncle could have paid, but that wasn't the case. All the bills very given to B.

Instant anger erupted from me. I could feel my ears and cheeks turning red. Most of all, I was tired of this nonsense and before B could stop me, I snatched the bills out of his hand and stormed downstairs. Before I entered the house I got a swift smell of delicious chicken tikkas and kebabs being grilled. More anger and irritation swept through me, as we struggled to make ends meet and they were enjoying delicious expensive food.

I threw all the bills toward Carl's face. I yelled at him to go get a job or go back to US. Everyone was startled with my behavior. In all these years I had never shouted or yelled at anyone. Uncle snatched the bills from his hand and threw it back on my face. He pointed his finger at me saying, "This is my house; he is my son and I will feed and take care of him as long as I want. How dare you come down and talk to him like that."

I snapped back at him, saying, "Behram is also your son who works at least twelve hours in this scorching heat, you don't feel bad for him.

"You three are also living in this house. Why is it only our responsibility to pay for all the utilities? You never had a problem before?" Then I stormed off.

I sat on the top stairs of my house, and I began to cry. It turned into a sob that kept going until my tears dried up. With my face in my arms, I found myself asking God the same questions again. WHY? You watch everything in silence yet you are not helping. What is it that you want from me?

The next day I apologized to Carl and Naz for my abrasive behavior. I always got along with both of them and didn't want any bitterness or conflicts between us. Carl also apologized and said I don't blame you. I should go back to US before my green card expires. In about a month, he returned to the US, leaving behind a young pregnant wife.

I felt sorry for Naz. She would have to wait for many years until she would be in US. Carl had a green card and could only sponsor her after he received his citizenship. That would be approximately five to six years.

Naz was totally dependent on Uncle for everything.

It made my heart ache to see her living like that. I had to step up for her many times and implored her to speak up for herself, so she didn't get verbally abused and manipulated like I'd too often allowed myself to.

One day she came upstairs sobbing. She couldn't even talk for a few seconds. After she calmed down, she said, "Today Papa took one bite of the food and said it was terrible. Then he pushed the plate away."

Instead of sympathizing with her I started laughing.

I said, "GIRL! I have been in your shoes for a long time. Keep him hungry for two days he will stop complaining." Then I told her a funny but true story. I said he used to complain about my rice every day. It was either soggy, salty, or tasteless. Even if it was perfect, he complained. So, I stopped giving him rice for two weeks. Whatever I cooked, I only gave him bread and naan.

After two weeks he asked B, "You don't eat rice anymore?" B answered that we mostly eat rice since the kids prefer rice to bread. He said he hadn't eaten rice in more than two weeks. B asked me about it and if I'd done that on purpose. "Yes," I said, owning it loud and proud. An explanation followed: I couldn't handle his complaints and insults and that made me feel better. It solved the problem too.

I am glad that I taught the complainer a lesson to appreciate what was given to him. When Uncle returned to rice, he was always complimentary, telling me I made the best kind.

CHAPTER 13

When B found that he was going to be out of work, due to the tumultuous environment of the Port of Karachi being privatized, he decided to join his dad at the nursery. They could expand that business and hopefully earn enough money to support both our families.

B started to take on landscaping projects at offices, clubs, and private homes. I had started tutoring children at home so at least we didn't have to worry about their monthly tuition. B was getting enough work but the Karachi violence affected everything. Just like Dad struggled with clients not paying on time, likewise B faced the same issues too.

Since B had two nursery plots and the upkeep was getting difficult he sold one for Rupees 4 lakhs, which would be around $4,000. It wasn't a large amount of money but it was substantial to us at that time. As many money problems as we had, B and Uncle decided to invest that money in bonds.

In July of 1999, Aunty returned to Karachi for a few months. Before she arrived, B requested to his dad not to mention anything regarding selling of the plot or money invested. B knew if Aunty found out she would cause unnecessary drama and tension in the house.

A few days after her arrival, B and I noticed they both were acting strange. Even B's aunt was ostracizing us, but we didn't ask about it.

Saturday, August 7, 1999, I was tutoring children. It was close to 1:00 p.m. and two children were left to be picked up. I was standing near my dining table and saw Aunty climbing the stairs in a huff and puff. She swung my front door open and came marching toward me.

A parent was standing near the table waiting for her daughter to pack her bag. She started shouting in front of her. "Where is Behram? He was supposed to pick up Uncle from the nursery. The poor disabled man must be so tired and hungry. Shame on you two for treating him poorly."

I was clueless and embarrassed with her behavior and told her very politely where B was and that he wasn't late getting Uncle.

She ignored my words and began to lash out at me for the way I treated her husband. I didn't focus on her words as much as I cared about her not scaring the children that were in my presence. I said we'd talk later and she raised her hand like she was going to hit me but at that moment another parent came in, so she left.

My heart was pounding and I was appalled by her accusations. What on earth was she talking about? She should have been thankful to B and I for tolerating Uncle's bullshit.

Twenty minutes later, I heard B's car and voice. I ran to the window. Aunty was by the gate, already shouting at B. She was roaring like a crazy woman about how irresponsible we were. B was caught off guard with her shouting. Irritated he asked, "Have you lost your mind?"

B said, "This is our normal routine." He was confused, his dad silent. Uncle quietly got out of the car and started walking toward the door on his crutches.

B looked at his dad and said, "What is the problem?"

Then Aunty started verbally abusing B and it was the most awful language I have ever heard. I was watching all the commotion and wondering what was going on. Then all three went inside the house. I could hear them screaming at each other. I asked Shad and Rowi to stay upstairs and I went down to see what was happening.

When she saw me coming down the stairs, she came outside with her hand raised again ready to hit me.

However, B came between us. Aunty looked like a crazy person who had no idea what she was saying. She was yelling at me for keeping Uncle unhappy, starved, and not looked after.

Aunty and B kept arguing and shouting back and forth until I lost my patience and tolerance. I started to yell back at her. I had no clue what she was talking about. I asked from which angle did the man look starved. Then I told her that if she was so worried about him she shouldn't be leaving her disabled husband in my care. He was not my father, brother, or husband, and not my responsibility.

Uncle was her responsibility.

I turned to Uncle, shocked and dismayed. "I don't know for what reason you have lied to Aunty, what you would gain from it, but let me tell you something, you have been unkind, selfish, hurtful but yet I have taken care of you for over ten years now. I didn't expect anything in return but just your respect and kindness."

ALAS! The truth came out. Aunty finally said that we had sold our nursery plot and had not given Uncle his share.

B and I were bewildered, shocked and aghast.

B was in tears when he heard that and said to Uncle. "You should have asked me, and I would have given it to you. But at least don't lie about something we haven't done. This is why I told you not to tell Mom about the plot because she would cause a fight and take money away from us."

Then he said to his Mom that every penny he had invested into the nursery was his. All his years savings were spent on the nursery, and she would not get a penny of it because it didn't belong to her. He didn't need to explain either. He had invested in certificates, just like Papa asked him to.

Aunty wasn't ready to hear anything. She yelled and abused B. "I want your fathers share of the money." B said, "Do whatever you want but I am not giving you anything, as its not yours."

The fight grew uglier and I tried to drag B out of the house, but instead Aunty caught hold of my shirt from the back and pushed me aside. I was completely startled, mad and in disbelief. Aunty shrieked at me that I would suffer and be miserable every day of my life and have worms in my mouth and stomach.

Uncle was quiet and observant. He didn't say a word until he looked at me and pointed his finger to me. "Behram was going to give me my share, but she wouldn't let him."

I got in his face, hysterically crying. "Say whatever you want. You and I both know this is not the truth. God will never forgive you for accusing B and I for something that we have not done."

Uncle became quiet, but Aunty came and pushed me on the floor. I remained on the floor, still hysterically crying, teetering on a total nervous breakdown. B tried to console me, but Aunty kept pushing me with her leg and kept saying. "Get out! Go upstairs and cry. I don't want all this crying in my house."

I couldn't take any of what was happening any longer and did run upstairs. I went to my kitchen, locked the door, and took out the sharpest knife from the drawer. I put the knife on my wrist but just couldn't cut myself. I don't know who was watching over me, but I thought of the kids. I didn't want them to be scarred forever. My head was pounding, I felt dizzy and nauseous. I just laid on the kitchen floor feeling weak and crushed. B nervously banged on the door, not knowing what was happening inside the kitchen. Though I was still dizzy, I managed to unlock the door and fell back on the floor.

The emotional abuses, curses, humiliation didn't stop for a few weeks. Uncle had stopped going to the nursery and stayed home all day. They depended on B's aunt to bring groceries for them and take Uncle to his doctor's appointments.

One day shortly after all that turmoil. B, Shad, Rowi, and I were returning from my parent's house. We had to enter the main compound to go upstairs. She came out and yelled, "Behram, are you giving us our share or not?"

B completely ignored her. I can't exactly remember what she had in her hand, but she started smashing all of B's expensive palm plants. B was shocked and ran to stop her with Rowi in his arms. Rowi started crying. I kept pulling him to come upstairs as I didn't want Rowi and B to get hurt. Then she said those terrible words, which no sane and loving mother would do. Only insane and despicable mother would. "BEHRAM, I WISH YOU DIE. I WISH ALL FOUR OF YOU DIE."

She didn't say it once but repeated it at least four times. I wanted to ignore her but after the fourth time I couldn't help but screamed back at her to leave the kids out of this. But just to spite us she said it over and over again.

I have never known anyone in my life as sadistic as her. How on earth could a mother and grandmother wish something so terrible to her own son and grandchildren; it was beyond my understanding. Her cursing, yelling, fighting never stopped, that's when B and I decided to give them Rs one lakh, as it was just not worth the fight.

I felt extremely sorry for B. He had put all his years of savings in this business, taken such good care of his father, went with them to Mumbai for his surgery, and this is what he got in return.

The next day B went to the bank, broke down the certificates, cashed out Rs one lakh, but before he gave them the money, he said. "This is Rs one lakh, which is much more valuable to you then your own son and grandchildren. Just for this amount you cursed us, lied about us. You have shattered our hearts. I might forgive you, but I will never ever forget."

B said to his dad, "If you think by giving Mom this money she will now stay in Karachi and take care of you, you are sadly mistaken. Trust me, in a few weeks she will leave again for US. Then you can call your other three children and ask them to take care of you."

* * *

Aunty went on a big shopping spree and began to spend all of Uncle's money. She invited family members to come for dinner and made their favorite dishes and desserts in their honor. No one interfered or said anything to Aunty, but Uncle's younger sister did. She told her brother what he did was terrible and he'd regret it. She was the only one who was incredibly angry with him and sympathized with us. The others just didn't want to get involved, which I understood—believe me!

After this incident B lost interest in the business. He would go to the nursery in the mornings, bring the kids home from school, and then nap all afternoon. In the evenings he would go to KPI, which stands for Karachi Parsi Institute. It's a club only for Zoroastrians.

We began to argue more, and I vented my frustrations on my children. As he grew distant, I was trying my level best possible to make ends meet. I would try and save every penny for tuition, but nearly every day he would ask for some cash from me for his cigarettes. If I declined, then all his frustrations would come out on Shad and me.

With so much going on in our lives, Shad being nine, was picking up on things. I got a phone call from his teacher one day to have a meeting. She asked me if everything was normal at home and I was honest, "No, it isn't." I didn't give her the details but mentioned that its difficult living with in-laws.

Shad had been getting into fights and hitting other children. The principal said the other parents were very concerned about their children and warned if that happens again, they will suspend him for a week.

More stress! I couldn't hold on to my tears.

Principal could tell from my face that I was tired and burnt out. She asked if I wanted to talk about anything, but I declined.

She put her hand on my shoulder and said, "Pray to Allah. He is the only one who can help you." I answered again, still wrought with emotion. "I do, but he doesn't listen."

By the time I returned home I was so emotionally and physically drained that, without thinking, I kept slapping Shad on his cheeks, head, shoulders—wherever my hands went on him. He tried to run away but I wouldn't let him and hit him even more. He was begging me to stop but I wouldn't. Until Rowi started crying, and I realized what I was doing. I sat on the floor balling, hitting my hands on the floor to hurt myself. Though Shad and Rowi were so young they still came and sat next to me, crying themselves and not understanding what the heck was going on.

I had not cleared from my first round of depression but this time it was worse. Nothing felt good or right, and I felt worthless. I had lost a lot of weight and now weighed less than a hundred pounds. I was having trouble retaining my food and purged almost everything I ate. I was placed on a diet to have more fruits, vegetables, and food without spices. The doctors couldn't find anything internally wrong, but stress and anxiety were at the root of my issues.

After all these fights, I locked myself in a closet. Except for my parent's house and family invitations I had to accept, I refused to go anywhere. I had just disappeared from the face of the earth.

Mehernosh saw my daily struggles and depression getting worse. I could tell it was difficult for him seeing his cousin suffer quietly but yet he didn't cross his boundaries and say anything to B, Uncle, or Aunty.

I would cry, pouring my heart out to him, but his sweet advice would always be to ignore them completely. I remember he always said, "You don't become like them by shouting back, because that's exactly what they want you to do. They want to hurt you and drive you insane, but you hold your head high and not say a word."

As I had mentioned before I hated reading books, but he insisted that I start with one. I can't remember which was the first one, but I became hooked on to true stories, not much of fiction and definitely not romance.

Every Sunday, Mehernosh would take me to our Zoroastrian Fire Temple to pray. At first, I was agitated to go and complained that God doesn't listen to my prayers. I wouldn't pray but just sit on the wooden benches but slowly I started to pick up our Avesta prayer book and pray.

He also introduced me to this wonderful lady, Late Katy Golwalla, who taught and guided me toward meditation with a special mantra. I started finding a little peace through prayer and meditation, plus some reiki sessions for inner peace and sciatica pain.

It had been a few months since I had any interactions with anyone from the downstairs house. I just kept myself busy with the house, kids, and my tutoring.

Whilst Shad and Rowi were playing with the other children in the park, Mehernosh would drag me out of the house to walk around the colony with other people. It didn't make a tremendous difference, but it was a good aversion for me. I even laughed a few times; never underestimate the power of a genuine laugh.

I will forever be indebted to my late parents and Mehernosh for being loving, caring, and supportive, both emotionally and financially.

CHAPTER 14

February of 2000, Mom handed me something that changed my life: a paid receipt and forms for Montessori training. She informed me that my class began in three weeks. Then added, "Whether you go or not, the money is nonrefundable."

I was ticked and argued that she should have asked me first. Well, Mom being Mom, she put me in my place. "Enough of your crying! Get a grip of your life, go for the training, and get a job. Enough of this crap of taking care of everyone. You are not their maid or nanny, you take care of yourself first, everything will fall into its own place."

Jeez Mom was mad and she was also absolutely right. I had wasted too much time and energy on people who were not worthy of my precious time. I needed to get out of the house and do something for me. Still, I was a bit apprehensive since we only had one car. How would B and Uncle go to the nursery? The training was about a forty-five-minute drive from our house, which meant I had to give myself about an hour each way to navigate the Karachi traffic.

When Mom told B about the training, she didn't ask, she firmly told him that I would need the car for classes. That he and Uncle would have to take the bike.

B didn't argue at all with Mom because most certainly everyone knew that Hootoxi had much patience, but once it expired, watch out! She also had a profoundly serious conversation with B, that they had kept quiet and not interfered for a long time, but now they were unwilling to tolerate any disrespectful behavior from him or his father, or they'd pack my bags up and take me and the children back home with them.

The training started three weeks later, and I became extremely busy with different projects. I had classes every day from 8:00 a.m. until 1:00 p.m., Monday through Friday. Afternoons were busy with tutoring and seeing to Shad and Rowi's studies too. By then Shad had started tutoring at our neighbor's house but I still needed to make sure he was finishing all his homework and assignments.

After dinner I would start with my own projects, barely keeping my eyes open. Life was surely testing my faith, patience, and sanity.

Aside from what I was now doing I still had to deal with the continual madness around the house, the latest being that the home was in poor condition.

B's downstairs house was constructed in 1969. Never having had repairs, it was falling apart, including Uncle's bathroom. The toilet leaked. Pipes were rusted. It was beyond repair—it needed to be replaced.

I wasn't willing to run short on funds for my household. Until that point, B had never asked for money from his siblings, but he was desperate. He swallowed his pride and ask his older brother for help but sadly B was turned down with abuses and asked never to call again.

B then requested his sister if she could help with $100 and she declined as well. (Hang with me, it is important to understand this for later on.)

I shouldn't have felt sorry for Uncle, but I did. Two of his children couldn't send him $100 or Euros. I knew they were bitter for what he had done but at the end of the day he was their father and had taken care of all their needs. I don't know how but B's cousin heard that his Uncle was having problems with his toilet and sent money immediately. Then in January of 2002, Uncle suffered a mild heart attack.

For once I was thankful Aunty was in Karachi. I was too busy with my new job at Links Preschool, tutoring, and taking care of the kids and house. After the 1999 fight, I didn't talk much with Uncle and Aunty. I only answered their questions with yes and no.

Whilst Uncle was still at the hospital, Aunty asked politely if I could stay with Uncle on Saturday. I wanted to decline but I didn't have the heart to. B and Aunty had been taking turns staying overnight. They both were tired and needed to rest.

The hospital was not private but government owned. The room was small, the couch in it filthy. I walked into the room and found him asleep. When he woke up, he was certainly surprised to see me. I ignored him mostly, but he kept staring at me and calling me over.

He put his hands in a prayer form, tears rolling down his cheeks. He couldn't even make eye contact with me.

He said, "Mora bacha" meaning my child, "forgive me." Tears kept rolling down from his eyes, his hands still in a prayer form.

I didn't know what to say and casually said, "Just get well soon. The doctors have asked you not to talk."

He rested his hands again and turned his face the other way. I felt nothing toward him, and his words didn't mean anything

76

to me. As the famous saying goes: "Sorry doesn't make a dead man alive."

He kept crying silently for quite a while and then fell off to sleep. But that didn't change anything for me. They had scarred me for life.

Not long after, it was Rowi's 8th Zoroastrian calendar birthday. B and I were getting ready to take the kids out for ice cream. Suddenly we heard Aunty screaming and shouting for help. When B and I rushed down, Uncle was on the floor, he had suffered another heart attack.

Aunty said he just finished his dinner and was about to go and wash his hands when he fell down from his wheelchair. He was conscious but he was holding on to his chest and in lot of pain.

We called for an ambulance, but no one answered. Luckily, B's cousin was at our house. Whilst the boys were putting Uncle in the car, I took the kids to Maneck and Bapsy's house to be watched. Aunty grabbed his medicines and previous paper- work, and we left for the hospital, only to be delayed by the heavy traffic.

Uncle passed away in the car, but we didn't say anything, knowing it was best to have the ER doctors check him out and release the news.

* * *

In our Zoroastrian religion, our funeral ceremonies are held depending on the time of death. Since he passed away in the evening his funeral was scheduled for the next morning.

In Karachi there are no funeral homes. Funerals are held in houses. Naz and I cleaned the house, rearranged the furniture, arranged all the chairs outside. B was arranging to bring the head priest to pray certain prayers before they would give

Uncle a bath. Aunty was still in a shock as everything had happened so fast.

With Zoroastrian funerals, mostly everyone wears white or lighter shades of color. I ironed a pale blue shalwar kameez for myself, cotton white shalwar kameez for Aunty, and a white shirt for B. The house for once was absolutely clean with lots of flowers, especially near his body. A diva, which is a flame, was lit, and charcoals were constantly put on the stove for the funeral. When the charcoals become hot, they are placed on a special vessel called the Afaganyu. Sandalwood chips and powder are placed on the hot charcoal, which gives off smoke and essence.

Seeing his lifeless body and pale face, I actually felt sorry for the life he'd chosen to live. I wondered what he learned, what he regretted, what he actually achieved. To me, his actions dug a big hole for himself. How sad he never got to meet his only son-in-law, daughter-in-law, and five grandchildren at that time. He never got to hear the news of Carl passing his Navy boot camp, coincidentally on his funeral day.

I reflected on our relationship as I watched his body lying there. Forgiveness had been granted but I'd never forget what he'd done to me. I lived with him for thirteen years, that's a long time to get attached to a person and have feelings. I attended all his prayers, helped in the kitchen, and did whatever I needed to do as a daughter-in-law, often doing so at the expense of my sanity and with tears. However, upon his death, I didn't shed one tear for him. There was nothing left in me to do so.

CHAPTER 15

A month after Uncle passed away, Aunty left for the US again. As for me, I was hoping it would be permanent. Since there was nobody downstairs, Aunty asked Naz to leave the house and live with her mom and brother. Naz left with her four-year-old son, Little Sammy, whom I absolutely adored. I would have supported and cared for her in a heartbeat, but my financial situation was also tight. To see her pack her bags and leave was heartbreaking.

After Naz left, it was finally just the four of us in the house. I had peace after thirteen antagonizing years and instantly felt much better. A heavy weight was taken off my shoulders.

Every morning before going to work, either I went for a swim to Karachi Club or workout at the gym.

I was less stressed, much happier, and a bit of my wittiness was coming back. It felt so amazing to rebound from those years of feeling like a caterpillar trapped in a cocoon. Now, I was finally a butterfly who was fluttering wherever I wished to fly.

I realized that in all those years, there was only one thing I was grateful to Aunty for. She had applied for our US immigration papers in 1989. We knew it would take many years, but it would be worth the wait.

But when the papers finally arrived in 2003, I was hesitant to make this big move. I was thirty-five and B was forty-three. My biggest concern were my parents and two aunts who depended on me for everything. With their aging came the need for us to take them to doctor's visits, get their groceries etc.

When I consulted my parents, without thinking of themselves or any hesitation, they said I would regret not taking the opportunity. They both said to get out of Pakistan and make a life for ourselves and our children.

And so the process began...

The immigration interview at the US embassy in Islamabad was in November 2003. To prepare for that, we had a list of things that we were required to obtain. Only one was a true obstacle: the affidavit of support.

Affidavit support is a document signed by an individual agreeing to use their financial resources to support the intending immigrant named on the affidavit. Nobody from B's family was ready to sign the affidavit and without those important documents we would never get our visas.

From my side of the family, the only close relative I had in US was Zarin. Zar had her in-laws living with her and dependent on them. I didn't feel right to ask her but a week later she called to ask if all the paperwork was ready.

I told her no one wanted to sign the affidavit papers and without that our papers will not be processed. Zar grew upset, wondering why I hadn't asked her. She said she'd sign the paperwork and we could come to Wichita and live with them.

I started crying, a burden lifted. I will always be very grateful to Zarin and her husband Jumby for stepping up for us when we truly needed family support.

* * *

August to November is not a long amount of time to prepare for immigration. There are so many details to tend to, from correct size and background of pictures for passports and green cards, police reports, medical records, and also selling our membership at Karachi Club and our Cyrus Colony house. Without selling these two valuable assets we wouldn't be able to afford our immigration expenses. Selling the membership was easy. The house was a pain.

The house was in B's paternal grandmother's name who was deceased twenty years ago. To make things more difficult we couldn't find her death certificate. B had to get out all the old documents and make her death certificate.

Then he had to take the papers to court to prove that Grandma was the mother of Uncle, who was also deceased, and then to change the owner of the house to Behram Irani.

For those three months it was so stressful for B and I, as we had a deadline to send all the documents along with the visa fees of $4,000. That is why selling the house was so crucial.

Houses in Cyrus Colony are strictly for only Zoroastrians. Since our community was so small and mostly young couples immigrating abroad, we knew it would be challenging to find a buyer.

Selling or buying a house in Karachi is different than in the US. No realtors, no closing dates, and no banks involved. The owner has to have his own personal money to buy a house.

The seller doesn't need to update the house even if it's in a terrible condition. We tried to negotiate the price, as there were two separate houses, but the buyer gave his final offer. Since this was the only offer, we accepted in desperation.

By end of April 2004, Shad and Rowi were done with school and were living with my parents. There was no point sending them to school for the month of May and paying for June and July as well. They wanted to spend time with my parents and that was a blessing to them, as well. B was responsible for finalizing the documents required of us. I was busy packing and selling our furniture.

Then there was Aunty, always something with that woman. She didn't want to know where we would be staying in the US, whether we needed any financial help, or if there was anything she could do for us. No questions asked about us, but B and I both knew it was matter of time and the question would come up. The time happened to come quicker than we'd anticipated it would. With a few days left before our move, Aunty called to ask, "What was the sale price of the house and when will I get my share?"

Just to see his mom's reaction, he asked her what share she was talking about. Nobody had put money into that house, from utilities to repairs to painting to taking care of Dad. He said he didn't understand what she wanted.

Whilst B was talking to his mom, I was getting irritated with him as I didn't want any more family dramas, nor did I want their share of money. In fact, I didn't want anything to do with them.

B's sister took the phone from Aunty's hand and said to B, "IT IS A MATTER OF PRINCIPLE. Everyone should get their share." These were her exact words.

He asked his sister where her matter of principle was when she'd been asked to pitch in $100 for her father's broken toilet.

B didn't have any intentions to keep anybody's share, he was testing them to see what they had to say, though deep inside he knew what their reaction would be. Once again, his heart was shattered because money was more important than her son and brother. If tables were turned and his siblings or my sister was starting a new life, we would have gladly given our share, but for that you need a big heart where money is no comparison to the value of family.

$3,000 was more important than B. It reminded me of the childhood story The Little Red Hen. None of the farm animals wanted to help the hen make the bread but they all wanted to eat it.

CHAPTER 16

May 26, 2004, we left our beloved country, family, and friends to start a new life in a different land on a different continent that we'd never even visited.

Since 1970, B's family had always left their front door key in the keyhole. After thirty-four years, B took out the keys and gave them to my parents to hand it over to the new owners. No matter what had happened in that house it was still painful for him to leave with all the mixed memories.

It was not going to be an easy road to start life all over again, but we wanted a better secured life for our children and for that we were ready to make sacrifices. I left Karachi with eight suitcases and four carry-ons, with basic clothes and kitchenware. The twenty-minute drive to the airport was filled with emotions and anxiety. I couldn't say a word. I had only ever been separated from my parents when Fara and I went to the UK for six weeks and when my parents were in Australia for a few months.

I had always been glued to them and knew that I would have some tough days to come, days where I missed them terribly. The same was true for Shad and Rowi.

At the airport, I kept hugging my parents, Khorsh masi, and Mehernosh. Life was unpredictable and I had no idea of when and if our paths would cross again, or even when I would be able to return to Karachi for a visit.

Rowi was only ten, too excited to travel and see her cousin Frea, but Shad was thirteen and had just finished eighth grade. He was not happy at all to leave Karachi, grandparents, and friends. He was at a tender young age where he didn't want to make this huge change in his life but of course I wasn't going to leave him behind.

Our long flight started from Jinnah International Airport to Wichita, Kansas. We had many layovers and had to be kept in specific areas for people "like us." We felt like monkeys in a cage. Why we were held there I wasn't certain but perhaps it was to check our luggage…over and over again.

After having our baggage checked in again, B and I sat near our gates but Shad and Rowi were too fascinated with all the shops and different types of people. They roamed around for quite a while, asked if I could buy them one bar of Cadbury chocolate and Smarties, which was the English version of M&M's. They promised to share equally. I thought, why not, but they didn't keep their end of the deal. In no time at all we heard them bickering about who ate more.

Finally, we arrived on American soil at Chicago O'Hare Airport. Everything looked, smelled, and felt different. It was like four aliens had landed in an unknown destination. Rowi immediately embraced it all and asked if we were at a mall. I laughed and said we were at the airport. She wanted to run around and explore everything, but we didn't let her, as we patiently had to wait until our documents were checked thoroughly. The Islamabad embassy had asked us not to tamper with the documents.

The seal could only be open by US immigration in Chicago. It took them four hours to go through all four documents. All four of us had to stand in front of them, for them to see the same people were travelling as on the document.

Thankfully, the last destination from Chicago to Wichita went seamlessly. We arrived in Wichita on May 27, at 9:30 p.m. We had been travelling for more than twenty-four hours.

* * *

The Mehta's and their cat Decker gave us a very warm welcome at their Bel Aire house. It was a cute and cozy home, way bigger than the one we'd left. It also had a beautiful deck with a big backyard.

In our honor, Zarin's mother-in-law, Allen aunty had made batasas for us. Batasas are biscuits made from flour and butter. They taste perfect with a hot cup of tea with mint.

We chatted for a while, saw their house, played with Decker, called my parents to let them know we had arrived, and then went to bed.

Though I was worn out, I still couldn't sleep a wink.

New places give me anxiety and my mind went in every direction besides sleep.

The next morning, we started filling out forms for social security and green cards. Without those it would be impossible to find jobs, open bank accounts, and enroll the kids in school.

Zar was an audiologist professor at Wichita State University and Jumby was the city manager.

To help us settle in, Zar had taken a few days off from work. We visited Shad's Heights High School and Rowi's Jackson Elementary. The kids were very fascinated that they didn't have to wear uniforms, they could dress upin their home clothes, they would get free lunch at school, and they could ride the school bus.

B and I were amazed as how everything was so systematic. The traffic was not crazy like it was in Karachi and everyone was diligently stopping at the signal light, which was a novelty for us.

At last, we got to see Walmart, a store that we had heard a lot about. It was mind blowing to experience a grocery store like Wal-Mart, which has everything under one roof. Unlike Karachi where we had to go to different stores, depending on what we wanted.

B and I had to learn driving on the left-hand side of the road and remember how to write the date as Americans did: month, date and year compared to date, month and year.

Petrol became gas.

Mobile became cell.

Dicky became trunk.

Drink became pop or soda.

And so many other words and spellings needed to be relearned.

The funniest one was when Shad asked someone in school if he could use her rubber, not having a clue what rubber meant in the US. The girl angrily asked what he meant. Shad gave her a confused look and pointed to the eraser. Then she laughed and said he was silly; the word was eraser.

We had never written a check or used a credit card before. In Karachi everything is paid in cash, even utilities. When Zar told us we didn't have to stand in line in the scorching heat to pay our utility bills, we felt like we had struck gold. Write a check and mail it. We were literally shocked. I did a happy dance as if I had won a million-dollar lottery. Only Pakistanis would understand that.

It had not even been a week in Wichita when Aunty called for her share of the money. She didn't even ask how we were doing.

B didn't want any dramas at the Mehta house. He tried to explain the social security cards hadn't arrived yet and when they did, we'd be able to open up a bank account and send the money. He said it was going to take a while and cautioned his mother that he wasn't running away with anyone's money.

By next week, B received his social security card, but they had made a mistake with mine at their end and had a delay. We needed both our cards to open an account.

Unfortunately, the phone calls didn't end. She called every other day screaming on the phone, that she had to pay for some dental work and was in dire need of money.

Aunty was making a fool of herself, no one believed her. She had always lied to suit her needs. Since we didn't have cell phones, she always called on the main line and left nasty messages for B.

It came to a point when one day Jumby had to speak to her. He said it very politely but firmly assuring her that the money is not going anywhere, she will just have to wait until everything gets finalized.

After a month, when we had our own bank accounts, we wrote five checks of $3,000 each and handed them to B's brother-in-law, who was apparently in Wichita for some work. B and I were not going to take anyone's share but it's sad just the way it happened. From that day onwards, the little bit of love that he had for his mom vanished into thin air.

CHAPTER 17

Since Zar was an audiologist, she mentioned some concerns about Shad's hearing. She asked us if we had him tested or noticed anything.

I jested with her that he is a typical teenager and gets deaf on purpose when he doesn't want to do something. But Zar was not joking, she was serious. She said that she'd noticed he didn't hear well, and also Jumby and Allen aunty had taken note of that same thing.

I didn't know how to cope with this new problem, so I kept ignoring and brushing it away. B had just started working for Target, we didn't have any health benefits yet: how would I get him tested? Fortunately, Zar did his hearing tests for free at the Wichita State hearing clinic.

The unfortunate news was that Zar had been correct; Shad had hearing loss and needed hearing aids. In all these years I had never noticed him having any difficulty and he had never mentioned anything to us. He did have the TV and music volume on high but that's normal with young kids who live on "the louder the better" mentalities—at least that's what I had convinced myself to be true.

It was heart wrenching for me to accept this problem. I wanted to ignore it and sweep it under the rug, but B explained that if we did that it would be difficult for him to cope with studies at school and later university. B was very sympathetic toward my emotions and guaranteed everything would work out. The hearing aid was going to costs us $4,000 but with Zar's clinic discount we had to pay $2,000. It doesn't seem a lot of money, all things considered, but at that time it was a tremendous amount of money for us.

Zar suggested to visit the Children's Miracle Network and see if they could help. When I went to CMN they said that since we are not US citizens, they could not help me. "What difference does that make?" I asked. After all, it was a child in need of help. I added that we were in the country legally and had green cards, and eventually would be citizens. My son was a fifteen-year-old innocent boy who was just diagnosed with hearing loss and they couldn't help because he was not an American. It made no sense.

One of the gentlemen said, "I'm sorry we cannot help you." But before leaving the room I had to add one last word in. "I thought this was a great country, but I guess I was wrong."

Without saying another word, I left the room with extreme anger. I went to the car dejected and hurt. I placed my head on the steering wheel and sobbed. I truly felt I was drowning everyday but still kept pushing my legs to stay afloat, but there comes a time in your life when you don't want to push anymore.

Whilst my head was still on the wheel, there was a knock on my car window. A middle-aged man wanted to know if I had paid for my parking, but then looking at me he asked if I was okay? I wiped my tears and just gave him a small smile. He smiled back and said everything will be okay. What a nice man, he didn't charge money for my parking.

Surprisingly, that evening I also received a call from Children's Miracle Network. They had agreed to pay $1,000 for Shad's hearing aids. The gentleman said normally they didn't do that for non-US citizens, but the board had decided to make an exception for Shad.

I was speechless and overwhelmed. I couldn't believe what I had just heard. Immediately, I thought of the man in the parking lot. He had said everything would be okay, and it was. It's hard to even express how very thankful I was to God and all the Angels who had helped us.

* * *

Throughout our three months stay with the Mehta's, I was always on the edge making sure the kids were on their best behavior. More scared about my firecracker Rowi, I kept reminding the kids to keep their volume low and not run around the house like they did in Karachi. Shad and Rowi were never fond of reading books or playing board games, they were my wild street kids who had always played outdoors with friends. This is what I was up against.

Every evening right at 6:00 p.m. Frea's grandparents religiously watched the local Wichita news. The three musketeers (Frea, Rowi, and Shad) decided to play coin games on the basement stairs. I kept reminding them to keep the noise down and they didn't listen.

Frea's grandfather couldn't hear the news and yelled at them to be quiet. Frea ran to her room, Shad hid in the basement with a Harry Potter book, but Rowi didn't run. Her hands were on her hips, whilst she stormed up the stairs pounding purposely on each step and said,

"ALL DAY BE QUIET, BE QUIET, BE QUIET!"

I was in the kitchen making tea when I heard her. I ran toward her and placed my hand on her mouth, dragged her into my bedroom, which was right near the living room, and pushed her down on my bed. I was so embarrassed with her behavior and ordered her to shut up immediately. But stubborn as she was, she just wouldn't be quiet.

I dragged her over to apologize but ran into opposition. Allen aunty couldn't stop laughing. She added that Jumby and her sister Lolita never had the nerve to say anything to their dad, not even Frea.

Frea's grandfather also started laughing, saying, "Those two ran away but this little one is a fighter. I'm glad she stands up for herself."

They were so nice about it, but I was still embarrassed. That child of mine knew no boundaries and had no filter.

By August of that year, we moved from the Mehta's house to a two-bedroom apartment near them. Schools were reopening after the summer break and we wanted the kids to have their own space, despite knowing they would have to share a bedroom. They didn't care as they were used to that. Our Willow Creek apartment was small but cute.

For months we ate and slept on the floor and dragged baskets of laundry to the common area where they had all their washers and dryers. Yet, it was good times. We had a small TV, which someone had given me from my daycare to check the weather and local news. The four of us ate, joked, and laughed until our stomachs ached. It brought back a lot of memories from my JB days. That's how I always imagined my own family would be. I wasn't interested in material things, all I wanted was my house full of love, peace, laughter with happy memories. It had taken fifteen years, but the small cozy house was "our home."

B worked at Super Target and after submitting many applications, I finally found a job at Woodland Lakes Learning Center. It was preschool in a church. It was not the kind of job I had in mind, but I couldn't be fussy because I had responsibilities to meet.

I was prepared for it to be a bit rough in the beginning but had faith that everything would work out. As long as I had B and the kids with me, I had nothing to complain about.

Before Shad started at Heights High, we met the Vice Principal who showed us around the buildings. Shad was surprised that the students had to go to the designated classrooms instead of the teacher arriving at their classroom. He knew he didn't have to wear uniforms but was surprised to see a few kids in their slippers with pajamas. He was amazed how the boys were allowed to have long hair with weird hair styles, their pants halfway down, showing their underwear. Their shirts were not ironed, and caps were allowed to be worn in the classrooms.

Girls had full make up, skimpy shirts and dresses, some without bras. All these things were new and fascinating. It was unlike anything Shad had seen before, or frankly, any of us had.

Schools in Pakistan were strict. Uniforms have to be ironed crisp; shoes polished. No jewelry except for small earrings, boys' hair was short and girls with long hair had to be braided using only black or brown hair pins.

Rowi was super excited that she could finally wear whatever she wanted and apply nail color too. However, when it came to clothes, I was strict with both of them.

They had to wear decent clothing, which was ironed daily with proper socks and shoes. I didn't care how the others were dressed but I made sure they were dressed appropriately, no matter where they went.

* * *

With each passing month we settled into our new lives more. I still got homesick and missed my parents. Calling them was expensive so it became necessary and easiest to email mostly and have a weekly conversation.

I was always excited to hear my parents' voices—that was the best way to tell that they were truly okay.

Shad and Rowi couldn't wait to talk with them about their school, new friends, and of course complaining about me.

Shad had joined the high school swim team and Rowi was in choir and band. She was learning violin. We wanted earplugs at the beginning. Wow! It was hard but in time her music became quite enjoyable.

On the weekends they both rode their bikes, played frisbee with the neighbors, and at times Jumby took the three kids to explore more of Wichita.

B became very busy with early morning shift work and in the evenings, he took HVAC classes at Wichita Technical School.

As months passed and cooler weather started in October, the four of us were freezing whilst the natives of Wichita said it was beautiful. That December of 2004 was our very first winter. It greeted us with an ice storm. The combination of snow and ice was something we had never experienced before.

B had to be at work by 4:00 a.m. that morning and the two of us got up at 3:00 a.m. just to clean off our car. B started the car, but the thick ice wouldn't melt. Our neighbor who was also leaving for work saw B and I struggling and gave us an ice scraper, de-icing fluid, and a brush.

Our neighbor didn't ask where we were from but said with a laugh, "You guys are most certainly not from Kansas." How right he was!

Everything was a new learning experience for us, whether it was cleaning the car after ice storm, to driving, banking, car washes, and even drive-thrus. We were learning to adapt a whole new system at ages 44 and 35.

CHAPTER 18

After two years of being gone, in the summer of 2006, Shad, Rowi, and I went to Karachi. Normally people travel to Karachi during winter months, but since the kids had long summer breaks and I had left my job at Woodland Lakes, it was best to go for eight weeks, not two.

Most flights from US to Karachi arrive in the wee hours of the morning. As usual my lovely Roshan aunty and Chum uncle had come to receive us.

My parents were ready to see us and spoil us. The first thing they had for me was a hot cup of tea with mint and Yazdani bakery's fresh bread with butter. Mom had asked the breadman to bring fresh bread from the last batch of the day. We savored that bread until the last crumb was eaten.

For the two months we were there we were pampered with delicious and scrumptious food. Thrity masi and Khorsh masi would send over marble cake, cottage cheese, fresh fish, and all of our favorite dishes.

It didn't take long for me to be reminded of my silly dad's wittiness. Taking our names, he would ask our cook Jamna to make his special sweet dishes. But Jamna has been with us for years and she knew exactly what each of us liked and disliked and knew it was not our favorite, but Dad's.

Roshan aunty would send her special fried fish, sweet yogurt and ravo, which is made of semolina, eggs, and milk. A delightful, sweet dish with fried almonds and raisins on top. It was Shad's and my favorite sweet dish.

After years I had a wonderful holiday of just eating, relaxing, and watching Bollywood and Pakistani soap dramas with my parents, not forgetting gallivanting with my friend Polki in rickshaws. Shad and Rowi were out most of the days with their friends, either at their house watching movies or at the beach.

It was such an amazing time, and a big part of me was rather sad to have it end.

* * *

Eight weeks of a lovely vacation flew away too fast.

I didn't want to return to US, but I had to. Shad and Rowi would soon be starting school again and I needed to find a job.

I updated my resume and mailed many applications to different schools. After a week I was called for an interview from Wichita Montessori School. The sweet kind lady on the phone said, "Dear, I'm so sorry but our air condition unit has conked out, I hope you don't mind, but you can wear shorts and T shirt if you want." Not knowing whom I was speaking to I fell in love with that woman.

Wichita Montessori School impressed me from the first moment I arrived. I received a warm greeting from two women: Mrs. Karen Combs and Mrs. Barbara Foreman.

After introductions, Mrs. Combs gave me a pat on my shoulder and said, "Why are you all dressed up, it's so hot."

I knew this was the woman I had spoken to on the phone. I laughed, sharing that I had just returned from Karachi, so comparatively this is beautiful weather, not hot. Both the ladies were in cotton T shirts and shorts, the door was open, and wind was blowing but they were still sweating and couldn't believe I was sitting so comfortably without a drop of sweat.

Mrs. Combs asked about Karachi and how life is different on the other side of the world, what brought me to Wichita, my family, and education.

I was nervous before I met them, and in no time at all it felt like I had known them for years. It didn't feel like an interview, it felt more like a general conversation that lasted for two hours.

When I left, they said they would call me within a day or two, as they had received other applications.

However, an hour later they called back and asked if I wanted to join their team.

I was super excited. I asked her if I could join them immediately instead of end August so that I could get to know other teachers. She said very politely that my pay would not begin until school started, was I sure? Yes, I was sure. I wanted to get to know the teachers and help in any way I could. That particular day in July I didn't know I was making friends forever.

Come Monday I was introduced to all the teachers of WMS. Each amazing and special. Upon my introduction to one of these women, Mrs. Indranie, I was in awe. She had been trained by "the Dr. Montessori" herself. Yet, when we talked her questions were not about Montessori.

Are you from India? *No, Pakistan.*

Do you watch Bollywood movies? *Oh absolutely, I am the Queen of Bollywood.*

Have you watched Bollywood movie Biwi Number 1?

98

I wasn't sure if it was a test, but I do know that we talked about actors, nothing Montessori related. It was hilarious.

I officially started WMS on August 23rd, 2006. I quickly learned that I was the baby of the school—the youngest staff member. Admittedly, it took a bit of time to get used to a few of the women but in time, we got along very well.

Being new and relatively young, I tried to find my own space and identity. Mrs. Indranie took me under her wing, and I worked with her very closely in Math. Though I had learned all the presentations in my training I still wanted her to teach me the way Dr. Montessori had taught her.

Mrs. Indranie was a lovely kind woman but a stickler when it came to presentations. I remember her asking me to give a teen board lesson to a child. I know she was watching me like a bald eagle eyeing its prey. After the lessons she said I did good with the content but my back wasn't straight. I know I rolled my eyes when she wasn't watching. Maybe I was a kid!

* * *

October 2006, we moved into a four-bedroom house with three bathrooms and a three-car garage, plus a huge back yard that faced east. The home had a nice size kitchen with a dining area that opened up to the living space as well. Shad and Rowi were excited to have a bedroom of their own, especially Shad, as he got the whole basement to himself.

Well, we had a house—finally—but we had no furniture except for beds. Mrs. Indranie had given us her old couches and love seat, which was perfect. More than furniture, purchasing a washer and dryer was necessary.

After two years of dragging heavy laundry baskets and detergents in snow and rain this was truly a big blessing.

99

Rowi settled very well at Stucky Middle School, whilst Shad was a victim of bullying at Heights High. He was bullied because he was from Pakistan and wore hearing aids. Few boys on his swim team called him Osama Bin Ladin, and repeatedly told him: deaf Paki go home.

They found every opportunity to degrade him in front of others. They would purposely ask him if he owned a car or if he traveled by a camel. Such ridiculous questions just to mock and disrespect him.

Shad was unhappy and hated being in the US. He missed his grandparents, friends, and always insisted he could go back and live with my parents. I could see his frustrations as he had never been treated so poorly. He even wanted to quit the swim team. His friend, Bo Beins, convinced him to stay and face these challenges instead of giving up. Bo was two years older than Shad and a fantastic swimmer. He would take Shad to all the swim meets in his own car so Shad didn't have to ride with the other boys.

But after Bo graduated, Shad had to face these boys one more year until he graduated.

One day Shad came home, extremely distraught.

His cheeks and ears were red with anger. He threw his bag on the floor and shouted, "Why did you bring me here? I want to go back home and stay with granny and grandpa. I don't want to live here anymore. It was your choice to bring me here, not mine. I was happy in Karachi with my friends."

I was so distressed seeing Shad like that; the pain and anger were hard to take in. At age sixteen, being a sophomore is difficult but to be an immigrant Pakistani trying to make friends and fit in with his peers was onerous.

Rowi was watching her brothers anguish quietly. After Shad had calmed down a bit, Rowi rolled up her sleeves as if she was ready to fight. Snapping her fingers she said, "Shad, give me the names of all the boys who bully you." Still rolling up her sleeves and fixing her collar, I reflect on this and wish that cell phones would have had video in those days. It would have been great to record the whole event; it was actually too cute and funny.

Shad still red in his face, snapped at his sister and asked, "May I know what you are going to do?"

Rowi said, "Oh you just take me to them, and I will punch their faces."

Shad said, "Rowi, have you seen their size? They will flick you off like a "machar." Machar means a mosquito in the Urdu language.

By then Rowi had her hands in a fist and bouncing as if she was a heavy weight boxer. Shad grew more irritated with Rowi, yelling at her to shut up. Rowi said, "Fine don't take my offer and keep getting bullied." Rowi stomped out of the room, and I just couldn't stop laughing.

Actually, Shad couldn't help but laugh too. He pointed toward her bedroom door and rolled his eyes. "Ya, for sure she is going to fix them."

My sweet precious Rowi who weighed ninety pounds and was 5'3" would have needed a ladder to punch those boys. Her punch would have felt like a tickle to them. If Rowi would have been at Heights High at the same time, she would not have hesitated to set those boys straight. Her physique was small, but personality was strong and powerful. Rowi had never shied to speak her mind or argue especially if she was right.

CHAPTER 19

On the whole, Shad and Rowi were good kids, but their biggest problem was they were not morning people—just like their Fara masi. Out of five school days, they would miss the bus at least twice or thrice, especially Shad. Missing the bus meant I had to drop them off at school, which was the opposite direction from my work.

One day I had enough. He missed the bus again. When we pulled up to Heights High, I didn't leave him at the main door but went toward the parking lot. He asked me with a nonchalant expression, "Why are you parking?"

Without answering his question, I got out of the car and started walking toward the main building. Shad was out of the car and walking right behind me. "MOM. MOM." I wouldn't answer. That day he knew he was in trouble but didn't know what I was about to do.

When I entered the building his vice principal, Mr. Santos was standing near his office greeting all the students. He saw me walking toward him with Shad at the back, head down.

Mr. Santos said, "Good Morning, Mrs. Irani. Today you seem to be in a very good mood." Of course, he was joking. He asked what he could do for me?

I said, "Mr. Santos, this son of mine doesn't wake up on time, misses his bus, and then I have to drop him to school and get late for my work. This has been going on a long time and I cannot do this anymore."

Mr. Santos chuckled. He put his hand on my shoulder and with the other hand took out a card from his pocket, which had his cell number.

He said, "Next time Rooshad doesn't get up on time you just call me, and I will pick him up from his bed. He will not have time to brush his teeth or change his clothes."

Shad's head was still down, he was angry with me and embarrassed. Yet he knew—without a doubt—that if he didn't wake up, I would most certainly call Mr. Santos.

It turned out that wasn't the toughest situation Shad would face. During his senior year, Mr. Silva asked me to come to school immediately. I had no idea why. But when I got there all he said was, "Rooshad is fine, but I need to see you."

It was a good twenty-minute drive and I just couldn't understand what was wrong. Mr. Silva was waiting for me in his office with Rooshad, who was seated opposite him with his head down.

"Mrs. Irani, I am absolutely shocked and disheartened that Rooshad punched two of his swim team friends. I have known Rooshad since his freshmen year, he is a very good kid, I just don't understand what happened."

"Mr. Silva, I am very sorry regarding his behavior, but I am not surprised. Rooshad has been bullied since his freshmen year and has been called horrendous names. They have never physically hurt him but emotionally they have.

"Rooshad had many times complained to the swim coach, but no action had been taken against these boys. The reason why no action was taken because those boys are excellent swimmers."

I went on to say that I had wanted to come to school to fix this problem, but Rooshad didn't want me to, he said if you intervene things might get worse.

Mr. Silva asked Shad what did they say to you that you punched them?

Shad finally spoke up and said, they called me terrorist and asked me to go back to my country.

I could see Mr. Silva's face getting red with anger.

He apologized to Shad and me and regretted what had happened in his school.

I don't know what actions were taken against those boys, but the bullying stopped. Since it was Shad's last year at Heights, he stuck it out but was absolutely ready to graduate and get out of there.

I felt sorry for Shad. His high school experience wasn't the best.

* * *

When kids cannot drive you crazy enough on their own, add a dog into the mix. Max was our mischievous, charming, fat, lazy but hilariously adorable pug. He was fawn in color but had a black forehead with wrinkles. He slept on Rowi's twin bed, taking much of the space, leaving a tiny spot for her. He snored and scream barked if he didn't get his carrots or Chipotle chicken, which Rowi tried to sneak in without him knowing. It never worked.

Sweet and spirited Max loved to run around the house, going in every room at least four to five times before settling down for a nap. When Rowi took him for a walk, halfway through it he would lie down and refuse to go any further.

Most of the time Rowi had him on her hip like a baby, laughing as she complained about how ridiculously lazy he was. Our Fatty, as we lovingly called him, was a scapegoat for all of us. He was always put in accessories like headbands, tutus, a scarf wrapped like a hijab or a Hawaiian flower. He absolutely tolerated all our nonsense giving us the cute innocent puppy face. Though Max was never allowed on the couch, he sneakily slept on my dining chair, all rolled up, thinking we couldn't see him.

Let me tell you, chaos happened every Saturday with Shad, Rowi, and Max, without fail. Shad worked on the weekends as a lifeguard at the North YMCA. He worked from 4:30 to 8:30 a.m. So, while Rowi and Max were snuggled in bed, Shad would take his annoying whistle and start blowing in Rowi's room.

Rowi would start shouting at Shad to stop and to get lost. Of course, Shad didn't stop. He just blew the whistle louder and harder, leading to Rowi screaming and Max barking.

Rowi would then jump out of bed and try to hit Shad, who dodged her by running around the dining table with Rowi behind him yelling and screaming, and Max running after both of them barking his head off.

I'd look at their Saturday shenanigans and wonder when our house might ever have sane people living there.

At that time, I used to get irritated and asked them to shut up, but today I would do anything and everything in a heartbeat to have that noise and chaos back in our lives.

One never realizes how much they miss these small moments of chaos, which are truly the blessings of a loving household.

*   *   *

May 2008, Shad graduated from Heights High School. Shad didn't want to join WSU right after High School. He didn't know what he wanted to do and just needed a break. Despite his pleas we still forced him to go to Wichita State —and yes, I now feel that was a mistake. He should have been given the chance to take one semester off. Shad miserably failed in both his fall and spring semesters.

By October of 2009, B's brother Carl who was in the military received a new post in Hawaii. That inspired Shad to see what options he had to join the US Navy or Coast Guards; however, his hearing loss made it impossible to clear the medical exam. He still went to Hawaii for a visit.

When Shad left for Hawaii, Rowi was a freshman at Heights High. Queen Rowi was too spoiled by her dad and bro to take the bus. Either one of them would drop and pick her up from school. When Shad left for Hawaii, B dropped and picked her up. Then B decided to leave for Hawaii for a bit, which made Rowi's heart drop. Drama Queen Rowi said to B, "Are you seriously going to leave me with Mom? You know she will torture me."

B said, "Now Rowi, you are being silly and dramatic. By no means is your mom going to torture you."

She reminded Dad that she'd be forced to ride the bus and eat vegetables.

And Rowi was correct! I made her ride the bus, cooked lentils and vegetables, made her eat fruits, no sodas or coffee, which her dad had never refused her Highness.

But at the same time, we had a lot of fun too. We watched movies until late at night with chips and popcorn, baked brownies and lazed around in our PJs all weekend.

Nobody doubted that I was the main disciplinarian of the house, too strict and not as fun as I should have been. I was raising my children the way I had been raised. Only in reflection, I think about my rules and wonder what difference would it have made if they didn't make their beds as soon as they woke up, not a bit later. Rowi always wanted to have her hair colored and I never allowed it.

What was the big deal, she was just exploring like any other teenager?

Going back over the memories from my year's passed by, I wasted too much of quality time focused on others and their opinions. Nobody in this entire universe is more important than your own children. If only I would have understood that thirty-two years ago.

CHAPTER 20

January 10, 2010, I asked Mom how her doctor's appointment went. She'd been having some problems with breathing. Without any hesitation Mom told me she had stage 4 lung cancer. She was so matter of fact in the way she said it and I was responsive in the opposite manner, feeling like I'd just been crushed.

I was speechless. I thought I'd misheard her, or she was fibbing (although it was not funny).

Mom said, "Are you there or have you hung up on me?"

The only word that came out of my mouth was "cancer." How was that possible? For some reason, we always hear such things, but we feel it won't happen to us or our loved ones. But this was a reality: Mom had lung cancer, stage 4.

She said very calmly, "Oh don't worry, I'm not going away so fast. I will take chemotherapy and will be fine."

Mom was talking as if she had a flu and could take something for it, then be fine. I wondered why it was not detected earlier. I kept on asking questions as I tried to process a reality I did not wish to accept.

Mom patiently answered my questions, then brushed me off. "You will be late for work, so you'd better get off the phone. We can talk later." Then Mom hung up, leaving me an emotional mess.

I crawled back in bed, clutching my pillow for comfort. I was angry with God yet again, this time for not protecting my mother and giving her one problem after another. Yet, Mom never wavered on her faith like I did. Nor did she ever complain but went with the flow. She prayed and bowed down to God but when it was time for her to enjoy the rest of her retirement life, she got cancer. It was unfair.

With Mom's diagnosis nothing seemed right. My heart and mind were in Karachi with my parents. It was only January, and I wouldn't have a summer break until May. There was only one thought that was bothering me. Will I ever see her again?

A few days later, Mrs. Combs and Jane pulled me in the office and asked how my mom was doing? Then they asked why I wasn't going home?

I became quiet but from my look she knew something was bothering me. Very reluctantly, I admitted my truth. "B and I both have to work to make ends meet."

Mrs. Combs said, "Go home and take care of your mom and you can return after the summer break. Your salary will be deposited in your account."

I was absolutely speechless and stunned. I couldn't believe what she was saying. I jumped from my chair and hugged Mrs. Combs and Jane and didn't let go for a long while. It was a release I needed and the only way I could show how I appreciated the offer.

With unstoppable tears, all I could say was thank you to them a million times. Apart from my immediate family, no one in this entire world had done anything like this for me. AMAZINGLY WONDERFUL WOMEN!

* * *

This was the very first time I was travelling alone. As it is long flights make me extremely nervous and anxious. I didn't have a cell either, which meant I had no contact with my family for over 24 hours. When I saw Roshan aunty and Chum uncle at the airport I started to cry. Of course, my brave Roshan aunty said, "No darling, don't cry. Your mom is very brave, and you have to be brave too. God is great."

I had returned to Karachi after four years. I was most surprised to see the new construction of Shahrah-e-Faisal, originally known as Drigh Road. It starts at Jinnah International Airport and goes all the way to Hotel Metropole. Previously this road had many traffic lights but with the new construction it was one straight road with many underpasses and over heads too. After crossing Metropole hotel and coming toward the Saddar area everything was still the same. Sewage overflowing, more homeless people on the streets, pollution, power failures, garbage on the streets. But no matter what, Karachi was my birthplace and therefore, special to me.

It was only 4 a.m. but Mom and Dad were sitting in the living room waiting for my arrival. I didn't bother to take the suitcases inside; I just ran to give them a big hug. My parents had visibly aged and it made me hug them all the harder.

After putting all the suitcases in the bedroom, Dad asked if I wanted tea. I said, "Of course I want my mint tea with scrambled eggs, bread, and butter."

Dad giggled and said, "Okay, make it for everyone." Despite just ending a day plus journey, I was so happy to make that breakfast.

The next day Mom had an appointment with Dr. Nehal at The Agha Khan University Hospital. Roshan aunty joked on the way to the hospital that Mom had grown very fond of this doctor.

When I met him, I could see why this was so. He was extremely caring, polite, and respectful toward her. He took at least forty minutes with each patient, that's why everyone was late for their appointment. He wasn't one of those doctors who was only interested in making money, he genuinely cared about each of his patients.

Dr. Nehal suggested to try the medicine Tarceva instead of chemotherapy. Tarceva was used for lung cancer patients, but it was exorbitantly expensive—for rupees one lakh (about $1,000). I knew my parents didn't have that kind of money and nor did I. I kept quiet in front of Dr. Nehal but upon our return home I asked Roshan aunty how we were going to afford the medicine.

Without Roshan aunty's constant help and support I would have been completely lost. She guided me every step of the way on what needed to be done.

Roshan aunty asked me to write applications to each of the Zoroastrian charities and explain Mom's illness. At the AKUH, many patients use the Welfare Department to get additional discounts for doctor's visits and procedures like chemotherapy, radiation, etc.

There was a lot of paperwork to be filled out and even with the help of being on welfare it would not have been affordable if the trust funds wouldn't have kicked in. So, every time Mom had an appointment with Dr. Nehal and needed to do some blood work, I first had to go to the welfare office, wait in a long line, and get the paperwork approved.

Just a welfare card with the patient's name, photo ID, and their account number could have made life so much simpler for many families.

* * *

Mom's illness played an emotional impact on Dad and I. Dad was trying to be brave, but I saw him struggle to accept the situation. Mom had always been our rock-solid pillar: when that pillar falls the whole house tumbles.

Though Mom was quietly suffering, she never once complained or sulked about her illness. There were days she didn't have the energy to get out of bed but mind you, she still kept track of everyone, especially my dad, reminding him of everything he had to do for his own health.

On the last week of February 2010, Fara came for two weeks. I was so excited to see her because it had been nine long years.

It felt amazing to be with Fara and my parents—no kids or husbands. It was a rare opportunity filled with reminiscing about life, both the fun times and the fights.

Everything was great, until one day I heard Dad say something to Fara that broke my heart.

I heard Dad asking Fara to write another application to the Trust Funds for the second round of Tarceva.

Fara said, "Dad, since Toranj has been writing all these applications we can ask her, as she exactly knows what to write."

Dad's answer stifled me. "She doesn't write correctly and takes too much time."

My heart sank, thinking I'd misheard. Fara kept arguing with him about it. I hadn't misheard.

I went in the dining room, placed my hand on my sister's shoulder, and asked her to do the application the way Dad wanted. Then I fled for the solace of being alone.

Fara came outside and sat with me. She was sorry for Dad's behavior. I could tell she felt awful. I said to her, "I admit you have always been the clever one but I'm not that stupid that I can't write a damn application."

Stubborn as I am, I asked Fara to go inside and do whatever Dad was asking her to do. I was determined not to write the application no matter what Fara or anyone said to me.

I loved my Dad with all my heart and soul, but this was not the first time he had insulted me. His words broke my heart, especially at that crucial and painful moment.

My memories drifted to my first job at Links Preschool. I was going through a lot at that time. Both desperate for money and in need of some kind of experience, I hung on to this job as long as I could. I was not the only teacher that was unhappy. Our boss didn't have a kind bone in her body. She was arrogant and mean and only liked her specific teachers.

Links had started an elementary school in a new building. There was an open house where we could invite our family to tour. I had invited my parents to come but since Mom was at work, only Dad came.

After giving the tour we bumped into my boss, and I introduced Dad to her. She told Dad she was happy to have me in her school. Instead of saying thank you or a few encouraging words, Dad told her that he was surprised with her comments, as I didn't do anything at home.

I was tormented with his answer. I couldn't believe what he had just said, knowing too well what my life was like. I looked at him with teary eyes. It was such an awkward moment for me, I didn't know what to say, my boss didn't know what to say either, and could only offer a nervous giggle before excusing herself.

Dad disheartened me despite my love for him. I know he meant his stinging words to be funny, but he'd forgotten there was a time and place for humor, especially with someone he'd just met. After that, I didn't want to show him anything else. I picked up my bag and said, "Let's go."

We sat in the car silently. Only when I dropped him off did I speak. "Thanks for crushing my heart," followed by closing the door.

He thought I was being overly dramatic. All I wanted to know was why my own dad couldn't say a few nice things about me at times that mattered most.

All this reminded me that I was there for my mother, not to appease my dad. I buried my hurt feelings and ego the best I could to focus on Mom.

Regrettably, I did lose my cool. Ever since Fara had come she was giving me instructions about what I should do and shouldn't do, aside from the application incident.

Eventually she hit a nerve and I flipped out. "Why don't you leave your family for six months, take care of Mom and Dad, run around by yourself alone in rickshaws, sleep on the uncomfortable folding bed, and then I will tell you what you should do and shouldn't do." I continued yelling that every-thing was fine until she had come to Karachi, and she should just return to Sydney.

Mom, Dad, and Fara were aghast with my behavior.

I have never yelled at Fara in that manner before. Mom inter-vened and said to us, "I thought both of you came here to look after me, but you girls are fighting like cats and dogs. Both of you can leave. I can take care of myself."

Mom was absolutely right; we were there to take care of her and here we were fighting like spoilt brats. Fara was furious and offended. I did apologize sincerely. At first, she wouldn't talk to me or listen. A day later she was ready to apologize too.

Days later, Fara left, leaving me sad about the way the visit had ended. The first days had been awesome but when you factored in Dad's hurtful words and the mounting pressures, everything went haywire. It was a firm reminder that words spoken aloud cannot be taken back.

CHAPTER 21

Mom's condition was up and down. We had to take her to the ER several times for breathing problems and agonizing cramps. There were intense fevers and coughing up blood. She was suffering silently; however, I saw her pain and cried when I was alone at night.

Dad couldn't cope watching Mom in that state. He kept himself busy watching TV or reading his newspaper. By avoiding asking how she was, he felt everything was relatively normal.

One Sunday we received a surprise visit from my cousin Cyrus. Wow did her face light up!

She got up from the bed, went to her dresser to sit down and brush her hair. Only then did she walk out to the living room, arms stretched out to give Cy a great big hug.

Laughingly I said to Cy, "Ten minutes ago I was begging her to come and sit in the living room, but she said she was very tired but hearing your voice she jumped out of bed."

Cy jokingly said, "Don't be jealous because they love me more."

Mom sat for at least two hours, enjoying Cy's humorous company. He offered gossip of our Zoroastrian Community, his own workplace, or talked about our days when we were young and did silly things.

Other days, both Cyrus and Danny came to our house, talking about our mischievous activities of our youth, including our prank phone calls. We'd call the Beach Luxury Hotel and pretend to be Mr. Brown and Mr. Smith and book hotel rooms. In those days there was no caller ID or credit cards, rooms were just booked with phone calls. What wonderful days these were, filled with innocent mischief and being silly not hurting anyone. But these silliest pranks still fill up our hearts with good memories and laughter.

By May, Tarceva wasn't working for Mom anymore. Her health was declining fast and Dr. Nehal suggested to start with chemotherapy. She could have declined but she wasn't ready to give up yet. Then there were blood transfusions and lots of needles and blood work. Did she really want this? We did wonder and she thought about it, then said that if it was to happen starting the following week we needed to get her in with the hairdresser. She had to get ready.

I shook my head. "Seriously? A haircut and eyebrows." Mom gave me a startled look and said, "I cannot go for my chemo looking like this," pointing to herself.

I laughed, remembering how Dad wanted to be shifted in his private room because he wanted to watch Bay Watch. Now Mom and her demands? I most certainly had the funniest parents.

When Mom did start on her chemotherapy, and had some time to rest, I saw her get excited about one major thing. Shad and Rowi were going to be arriving for a visit.

I could see her strength coming back.

Dad was filling up the refrigerator and pantry with their favorite snacks.

Mom was ordering fresh marble cake, cottage cheese, batasas, date pies, and wafers.

Khorsh and Thrity masi had sent their favorite crackers and cheese.

The house was being spotlessly cleaned and new screens were placed on windows to avoid mosquitoes.

Mom took out her finest tablecloths, bedsheets, and comforter.

I joked with Mom that the royal family wasn't coming for a visit, just her two crazy grandchildren who will turn her house upside down. Her answer was expected: "My grandchildren are more important than the Royals."

I was so happy to see my Shad and Rowi after three months. They too were super excited to see their grandparents (and I hope me) and to be in Karachi after four years. They had already made plans with their friends as to what they were going to do for three months.

It had been a long flight, I thought they would be exhausted but they had all the energy in the world. I teased them that they must have had a nice airplane breakfast and couldn't be hungry. But both of them knew that their favorite breakfast would be ready.

I asked the kids if they wanted scrambled eggs but sadly their answer was, "Only if granny makes it."

Before I could say not to bother her with that, Mom jumped from her chair and went toward the kitchen to make them scrambled eggs.

I teasingly said, "You didn't even offer to make a toast for me, forget about an egg." Mom proudly said, "But you are not my grandchild."

Just by Shad and Rowi being there, I saw a huge difference in both Mom and Dad. In spite of taking chemotherapy and feeling miserable, she was ready to make anything the kids requested.

They had always loved her mango ice cream, cottage cheese, baked chicken with cheese, mango shakes, and of course her special secret scrambled eggs.

I'm so grateful and happy that the kids were able to make this trip. The house was not quiet anymore, it was filled with life and joy, ranging from loud music to the bickering that seemed like music, even to my ears.

That year we ended my time in Karachi celebrating Dad's 80th birthday on August 1, and then had to leave for Wichita. It was extremely heart breaking for us to leave but work and a new school year were waiting.

CHAPTER 22

Shad had his head straight and returned to Wichita State University in 2010 to study Criminal Justice. Our lives were chaotic at times and a bit crazy, yet we were happy. Until…THAT DAY in 2011! Shad mentioned that he was dating a Muslim girl. She was also a student from WSU.

I had absolutely no problem with Shad dating a Muslim girl. I have many Zoroastrian friends who are happily in relationships with Muslim men. However, when Shad brought her to our house my heart skipped a beat. My gut instincts were on high alert, and it was an uneasy feeling.

Dua was tall, pretty, and broad-shouldered with long wavy brown hair. She wore a hijab, something common for Muslim women to wear, and by all accounts she seemed normal and sweet. So why did I sense trouble?

After she left, Shad asked me if I liked her. I was direct because I'd wasted too much time not being that way in life. "Stay away from her; she is nothing but trouble.

Don't get into this relationship. You will regret it sooner or later."

Shad was surprised and angry. He shouted at me. "This isn't fair, you literally just met her."

I shared how something about the woman made me feel uneasy and I couldn't pinpoint it, but it was there. I added that I wasn't making excuses because she was Muslim; I just didn't have a good feeling.

Shad was extremely annoyed and irritated, storming out of the living room and stomping downstairs to his room. I followed him to try and speak with him but he wouldn't listen to a word I was saying.

My words didn't stop Shad. He still brought her to the house. Maybe he hoped that if I got to know her better, I'd change my initial opinion. I was polite and respectful, a good host if you will, but the off-kilter vibes remained.

Over the next months, my feeling didn't lessen or leave. My opinion remained uncertain. Her siblings began to show up too, which did not help. I was in a situation that was hard to handle.

To Shad, everything that Dua said was written in gold and whatever we said was thrown into the trash. But in spite of all this I didn't want to lose my relationship with Shad. I had to swallow a lot of shit from Dua and her family.

At times Dua would complain to me about Shad, she would think I was joking, but in literal sense I used to tell her. "Open the backdoor and run away. Far away from Shad." She would always laugh and say, "You are too funny!" I wasn't kidding though. I hoped she did that from the very core of my heart.

Many times, I tried to ease my own tensions by completely ignoring what was going on around me but I could only ignore it for a few days. I'd try to explain my concerns and Shad would just get angry and defensive—I was the dramatic one.

Mom's cancer. Now Shad. And next me. I began to feel off, not 100%. I felt worn out and started to suffer from migraine attacks, which landed me in the ER. My primary doctor advised not to visit Pakistan that winter of 2011 but to take it easy. But I couldn't do that. No matter what I was going through I knew I was needed by my parents.

The next visit to my parents was tough. Mom was even more fragile and thinner. Dad also looked weaker and tired. He had become quiet and didn't talk and joke as much as he used to. Mom's illness had created stress for my parents, which was stressful to Fara and me. We were always worried about what would happen after Mom passed away; how would Dad manage on his own?

One evening whilst watching TV, I asked Dad why he was so quiet and not himself. At first, he didn't answer and looked the other way. I could tell he was getting choked. After a while he finally said, "After Mom passes, I will be left all alone. I wish I would have died in 1995 and not survived the heart attack."

Hearing a parent say such things is gut-wrenching. Tears started rolling down my cheeks, I was dumbstruck for a few seconds, not knowing what to say to make him feel better. I held his weak weary hands and said to him that I was sorry I couldn't take him with me. Parents immigration would have taken a year but that was not the issue. The biggest problem was the health insurance. I promised him one thing: Fara and I will never abandon you. We will visit you, as we have over the years.

My words felt inadequate, my pain at his sadness intense. I suggested to take life one day at a time and enjoy each minute, hour, and day, instead of thinking what will happen after Mom passes.

As much as Dad didn't want to accept her illness, whenever we had to take Mom to the emergency, he wanted to go with us. We would ask him to stay home because we wouldn't know how long it would take at the emergency, but Dad would insist on being there, fearing it may be his last time seeing her.

* * *

The weather was absolutely perfect in Karachi. The sun was shining, birds were chirping, Dad was watching TV, and Mom was resting. I was sitting outside trying to destress myself. My heart and mind wandered in many different directions. What was different this time was that my parents weren't my main focus, Shad was.

I kept pondering if I was really trying to like Dua. The cloud of suspicion about her never was far away, no matter what I did.

I didn't realize Mom had been watching me from the bedroom window. She came outside, which was unusual for her, and asked what was bothering me.

I showed her a picture of Shad and Dua and said this is your grandson's new girlfriend. I didn't say anything to her, I wanted mom to give her own opinion.

Mom gave a glance to the picture and gave it back to me. She didn't ask me her name, about the parents or family, education, or anything. Not a word.

Mom was getting up to go inside when I asked her if she was going to ask anything. She shook her head and we never spoke about Dua again.

Shad asked me several times over the phone if I had shown the picture to granny and every time, I had some excuse for him. But when he asked again after a few days I said that I had.

Shad was excited. "What did granny say? "I showed her your picture, but she didn't say or ask anything. I'm sorry but this is the truth." There was a disappointment in Shad's voice. He was likely expecting his granny to share some kind words. It never happened.

I had never mentioned to anyone that Shad was dating a Muslim girl. But unfortunately, through Facebook pictures it was all over the world. Seeing her in a hijab, everyone knew she was Muslim. The most common question I was asked: Will Shad have to change his religion? I hated that question.

CHAPTER 23

Ever since Dua came into Shad's life things drastically changed around the house. Shad became more involved with her family that he almost forgot he had a sister and a house of his own. He became a little puppy trotting behind her and did whatever she asked him to do.

In just a general conversation I asked Shad, "What does her dad think of this relationship?"

Shad reluctantly admitted that her dad didn't know about them. That could not be good.

After knowing that her dad was unaware of her dating a Zoroastrian boy I was more uncomfortable. I hated the idea that she was sneakily meeting Shad at WSU and coming to our house too.

I kept pestering Dua when she intended to tell her father. I sensed he may be like us in that way, as he was Pakistani and wouldn't appreciate his daughter keeping such a secret.

Finally, I gave her an ultimatum: until your dad knows about Shad, you cannot be at the house unless B or I are home and you have to leave by 8 p.m.

It worked for a while but after a few days she reverted to her old ways. I always had to remind her to leave.

Shad was very bitter and angry. Our sweet relationship was getting sourer each day. We noticed he avoided dinners and started coming in late. When I asked him if he was at her grandma's house, at times he didn't answer or was rude, reminding me that they had to go there since she wasn't welcomed at our house. He'd always add, "You can't stop me from going there."

It was easy to see that I was fighting a futile battle, one designed to save him from making a terrible mistake. But he was headstrong and adamant to stay in this relationship. B, Rowi, and I were all unfond of Dua. Life grew tense; the situation became unbearable. I wasn't ready to choose between my son and Dua, so I put up with her more than I should have, just to offset some of her influence if nothing else.

We completely stopped saying anything to Shad. It all led to tremendous tension within the house and fights. Rowi was especially impacted.

At times Dua was nice and kind to Rowi and at times she would be unkind. Rowi would be spicy with her at times and sometimes remain quiet only for Shad's sake.

Rowi and Shad fought many days.

They got along others.

All I asked was that they be quiet when their dad was asleep.

Their level of kindness to each other was directly correlated to when Dua was around. When Dua wasn't around Shad and Rowi were best of friends. They spent a lot of time together, going to a movie or stopping by the QT to get their mango tea and chips and go for long drives.

They both shared a lot of secrets with each other and would never give the other away even when they were arch enemies.

They were my odd balls who chased tornadoes, had snowball fights, put crushed ice in each other's shirts and fought over the last ice cream cone and Oreo cookie. But no matter how much they bickered and fought, their sibling love for each other was anything but ordinary.

* * *

At Heights High, Rowi had also joined the Junior Reserve Officer's Training Corps (JROTC). It is a military regulated program designed to offer high school students leadership experiences and motivate them to become better American citizens. Though Rowi had no intentions of joining the military, she joined this organization with her friends, just to try it out.

When I met Sergeant Eric Yeager, I was excited and relieved that finally Rowi might learn some discipline and punctuality. A sergeant would not tolerate her nonsense and silly behavior. However, a few months later Rowi had drill with another high school. Before leaving the house, I asked her if she'd packed everything she needed, to which she responded with an eye roll and "yes."

Ten minutes before the meet was about to start, Rowi came running to me and said, "Mom, I forgot my shoes."

I rolled my eyes, shrugged my shoulders, and said, "Walk bare feet or go talk to Sergeant Yeager, as I am not going home to get them." Rowi was walking over to the sergeant, and I followed behind, admittedly a bit eager for someone to yell at her other than me.

When she told him about her shoes, he calmly said, "Oh, that's not an issue, Rowena, I have a few extras in my office; go try some on." I was startled, appalled, and dismayed. I asked him why she wasn't in trouble for not remembering to bring her shoes when he'd just yelled at another boy for forgetting his pins.

Sergeant laughed and said very calmly, "I can replace shoes but not pins."

I shook my head and couldn't believe what charm this girl has with everyone. Her dad spoiled her. I got it. Her brother did too, and I got that. But her sergeant?

Seriously!

Wichita was having its usual snow fall. Rowi asked her friend if he could take her to school. Rowi's friend was taking a ride with Sergeant Yeager and since it was on the way they would pick Rowi too.

Sure enough…when sergeant arrived she wasn't ready. Since the temperatures were so low, I invited him inside and apologized for Rowi not being ready. Mr. Yeager calmly sat in my living room for ten minutes, patient and polite.

I asked him again why he didn't leave without her. And guess what he said? "It's such a cold day, I understand she didn't want to get out of her bed."

I placed my hands on my face. I said. "OH GOSH PLEASE! She is not the only child who has to wake up on a cold day. Everyone spoils her. No wonder she doesn't take me seriously."

May 2012, Rowi graduated from Heights High School. Rowi and her friend Courtney wanted the whole nine yards for a celebration.

Rowi did have a wonderful graduation party.

Courtney's house and yard was packed with friends and teachers from Heights. There were pretty yellow and purple graduation banners placed in the yard.

Their cake was half yellow and half purple. Yellow is the color for Wichita State University for Rowi, purple for K- State University for Courtney.

Thankfully it was a wonderful day with no rain and thunder. All the kids were outside playing games, dancing, taking silly pictures, eating and make a mess of their melting snow cones.

As a graduation gift Rowi asked if she could visit Carl and Naz in Hawaii. Rowi was so ecstatic not only to visit Hawaii but also to see her favorite cousins.

Two weeks later Rowi's holiday came crashing as Aunty was also in Hawaii at the same time.

I was in Karachi when Rowi's crying phone calls started coming in. She called B in Wichita, begging him to book tickets and get her back. When B said I cannot do that, she would call me and cry.

It was very unusual for Rowi to cry. She was like me; she would bottle up as much as she could take and then cry when she couldn't take it anymore. I finally got some more specifics. Rowi asked, "Mom, am I not her grandchild too? Why does she love one grandchild so much and not me? She is rude mean and keeps insulting me in front of everyone. When I say something to her, then she disrespects Dad and you."

I understood how that woman could be frustrating, for sure, but I was so involved in my problems that I didn't have an answer. We hung up and I called her back a few minutes later. "Look, I'm sorry, Rowi. Just because your grandma is behaving so poorly with you doesn't mean you have to behave the same way, because that is not how I raised you, and most importantly not a reflection of your character."

I don't know how I did it all during those tough days. I was one person trying to take care of everything. Some days I failed and others I was victorious.

CHAPTER 24

Summer of 2012 was my next visit to my mom, and she had lost all her hair but never mentioned that. I wasn't prepared at all to see my mother without her thick wavy hair. I was dumbfounded and kept touching her bald head with quiet tears. The way I was holding her she knew I was crying.

She pulled me back so she could see my crying face and started wiping my tears. Mom said, "There is nothing to cry about. Think of all the money I am saving from haircuts and color. I have pretty scarves that can hide my head, everyone will think this is the latest trend."

I was so amazed with her strength and put my head in her lap with my hand around her hips and I just lay there quietly. She kept stroking my hair. It had been years since I had put my head in her lap. It felt so peaceful, and I cherished it.

I just lay there in bliss until she asked me, "Would you like me to make you your favorite scrambled eggs with cheese?" I looked up at her, so thin and weak but yet smiling. I couldn't decline her special offer. I felt it could be the last time I would be eating her special mommy scrambled eggs.

Since I had visited my parents in the winter of 2011, I couldn't afford to go back within six months. But since Khorsh masi had passed in February of 2012, Thrity masi didn't want to live alone in her big Parsi Colony house and wanted to move to Jamshed Baugh apartment.

Mom's youngest sister Shernaz Masi, who lives in Canada, said she would pay for my trip to Karachi if I helped Thrity Masi move. I left in May and Shad decided to visit around end of June. Though things had been rough and edgy between us, I was thrilled to have him without Dua. He helped me a great deal during that trip and I believe learned some things too in the process of helping Mom and Thrity masi.

When it came to Mom, her condition continued to decline. On many days her white blood cell count was too low for chemotherapy treatment, and instead plasma was given. I also had to give her shots in the stomach, which had to be extremely painful, although she didn't complain once.

Shad cherished spending each day with his grandparents, whether it was playing Carrom board game, cards, or accompanying them on their doctor's visits. For Shad, that visit would be his last to see his favorite granny.

A month after I left, Mom was admitted in the hospital for tuberculosis in a special unit. Dad and Roshan aunty went daily to see her but only Roshan aunty was allowed with the special suit, gloves, mask and shoes. She would go in for ten minutes just so Mom would know they were there for her.

By October, Mom was moved to the intensive care unit. One early morning Mom wanted to use the bathroom. She kept ringing the bell but nobody answered her call.

Frustrated by no one answering she got down from her bed but unfortunately fell and broke her femur bone. When Roshan aunty called and broke the news that Mom will be in surgery but under the circumstances the surgeon doesn't know if she will make it, I crumpled onto the kitchen floor and cried, utterly exhausted, both physically and mentally. I felt as if I couldn't do what I had been doing anymore. But what was most urgent was how I would ask for more time off and where would I get the money for the tickets?

I spoke to Jane that I might have to go back.

Without any hesitation Jane said not to worry about them, just focus on taking care of your mother's needs.

Once again what would I do without Zar and Jumby. They helped me with the ticket and on October 8, I flew back to Karachi.

After a long agonizing journey where I didn't eat a thing, we finally touched down in Karachi. I lifted the shades of the window and noticed the billowing clouds.

The sun was slowly rising and lent a yellow orange glow to the landscape. It gave me a sense of peace. Looking at the clouds, I put my hands in a prayer pose and asked God to please let me see my mom one more time and for her to know that I am with her. I placed my head on the window, closed my eyes, and begged for strength.

CHAPTER 25

A few weeks before arriving back in Karachi it had been under riots; violence was everywhere. Because of this and a fear of carjacking I didn't ask Roshan aunty to receive me from the airport. B's uncle did but not until a more respectable 6:00 a.m.

Though I had seen Dad two months ago we were so happy to see each other, yet visibly stressed and scared. We hugged tightly and he thanked me for coming again. "Your mom needs you and so do I. I'm sorry you have to miss work and leave your family."

I held his feeble hands in mine, telling him not to worry about us, we'd be fine, and they needed me now. Without saying it, I saw the look of relief on his face.

I didn't understand the relief my presence offered back then the way I do now. Children bring inner peace, strength, and a sense of love.

I went to the hospital as quickly as possible. When I entered the room, Mom was fast asleep, on her left side facing the window. Her left hand had two IVs flowing into her. One was for pain medicine and the other one was for her cancer. I don't know how she knew, but she opened her eyes and gave me a big smile from her oxygen mask.

I kissed her forehead and asked how she knew I was there. She didn't say anything but took my hand in hers and closed her eyes. I felt as if she wanted to kiss me but because of her mask she couldn't. She just stroked my hand and whispered she was glad I was there.

I met Dr. Nehal on his morning rounds, and he gently put his hand on my shoulder and said, "Your mom has been the best patient. Never whined or complained about anything. Its only because of her own will power she has survived for so long, but now very slowly her body is shutting down. We have blasted her with medicines, but at this point there is no point in any kind of treatment. Just pray that she goes peacefully and doesn't suffer anymore."

I hugged Dr. Nehal. Afterward, he continued. "You have gone above and beyond for your mother. Coming all the way from Australia and US is a financial strain to you both as well. Your mom is very lucky to have you both as her daughters. Not many people would have done that."

My tears flowed harder. "The number of sacrifices that Mom and Dad have given for us, this is absolutely nothing. Can't even compare."

Two days passed by and I had not rested or left the hospital. I asked Roshan aunty to go home and sleep, then I would after she returned. I just didn't have the heart to leave Mom by herself.

Just outside the ICU, there was a waiting room with many reclining chairs. Around midnight a nurse came and woke me up. She said that Mom was asking about me.

I followed the nurse to the ICU, Mom took off her oxygen mask, and pulled me toward her, making a hand motion to lay my head on her chest. She slowly stroked my hair, the exact same way she did when I was a child and sick. But after a while I saw her struggling to breath and I placed the mask back on her. I whispered in her ears, to go to sleep; that I'd be right outside.

She looked at me with the most loving eyes and fell off to sleep. Mom's condition was worsening every day, we didn't know if she would make it for another day or a few more weeks. Fara couldn't stay in Sydney and arrived in Karachi too.

And this struggle in and out of consciousness lasted for weeks. On October 30, I had to return to the States. I didn't want to and tried to change the ticket, but I could not afford what it would cost.

It was so hard to get on that airplane because I knew in my heart that I would never see my mom alive again.

One part of me was selfish and didn't want her to die, but the other part knew she was suffering, and she would be at peace. I had no way to say goodbye that felt adequate. I kept hugging, kissing, and touching her. I would leave the ward and then run back to her. I must have probably done this three times when Fara held me back and shook her head. I sobbed holding onto Fara and Dad, no words were spoken. I gave a last hug to Dad and left with Fara to B's uncle's house, as he was my ride to the airport.

I was super anxious leaving Karachi and wanted to be in US with kids and B, but when I reached Abu Dhabi they announced that the flight to Chicago was delayed due to Hurricane Sandy. I was so distressed. After seven hours of delays, I collapsed in my seat on the plane, exhausted enough that I was able to doze off for five hours.

On reaching Chicago I ran all the way to the United Airways counter and realized that I had missed my connecting flight. The lady at the counter said the next flight was at 9am the next day. I begged her to place me on any flight to Wichita but there was none at that time.

The lady was kind and -gave me her personal phone to call B. I was extremely anxious and nervous and couldn't settle down. B very calmly told me to get a hotel room for the night, a hot shower, and a good meal. That would help me to feel better.

I went to the room but wasn't able to unwind. Eventually, I did get home. That year, on November 14, Mom celebrated her 73rd birthday at Parsi General Hospital and passed away peacefully on the 17th. She was very fortunate that Dad was sitting right next to her, talking to Fara on the phone.

When Mom was shifted to Parsi General, she requested a picture of Fara and I to be in her room. When we'd call, she didn't have the strength to talk but Dad would press the phone to her ear so she could hear our voice. At the end of the conversation, I would always tell her "I love you" and she tried to gasp it back the best she could.

Mom was an Iron Lady. She was our nurturer, comfort, and home. It's because of her strength, morals, and values, I am who I am today.

* * *

Months after mom passed away, everything was still hurting. A cloud of gloom had swallowed me up. Nothing felt right. But I had to put on a fake smiley mask to show people that I was strong even though I was truly broken. I have always kept things bottled inside of me and barely vented anything to anyone. So, after Mom's passing, I struggled to deal with my own grief and Dad's immense sorrow at losing his wife. I was so entwined in my own web of problems that I didn't notice anything different happening in my own house.

CHAPTER 26

By 2013, Dua's father was aware of Shad. He was unhappy and angered that his daughter was dating a Zoroastrian boy and therefore he wanted nothing to do with Shad.

To me, he should have considered himself lucky his daughter was dating a Pakistani boy who was respectful, could speak and write Urdu fluently, and had a solid head on his shoulders. But the father's mind was only set on one thing—religion.

Shad respected his wishes and never went to their house, but what really irked me was that Dua was always in and out of our house, as if she was my daughter-in-law. She ate dinner with us, went shopping with Rowi—I mean argued with Rowi during shopping trips.

Shad started to act strange, which I didn't catch on to, but B noticed. He refused to eat pepperoni pizza—which he loved—and never had a beer with B while grilling. B cautioned me on his suspicion—that he was converting, or seriously considering it. The day B told me I was so upset with him and argued that Shad is stubborn and head strong but he would never do anything like that to us.

Six months later Shad and Rowi got into a huge argument. This wasn't one of their sibling arguments. Rowi told him to tell the truth and that she wasn't going to lie for him anymore. I went toward the kitchen and asked them what was going on.

Before Shad could defend himself, Rowi blurted out angrily that he had converted to Islam and that she was sick of these everyday fights and arguments in the house.

After she blurted that out in anger there was a pause; everything came to a freeze, nobody moved or said anything.

I looked at Rowi and said what did you just say? Then I whacked her shoulder and asked her why she's saying such a thing.

Rowi sat on the floor and became very hysterical and started shouting, "I'm not lying! Instead of hitting me why don't you ask him and hit him instead." Then she shouted at Shad to tell us the truth.

Shad couldn't look at me. His head was down and face red. I went up to him, caught him by his shirt, and said, "Please don't tell me this is the truth."

The words finally came out. "Yes, it is true. I have converted to Islam."

I was still holding his shirt and shaking him as I began screaming, hitting him wherever my hands could reach. He only stood there in silence.

B had entered the room and heard everything. He was not shocked but remained quiet. Seeing Rowi and I hysterical, he asked Shad to leave the house until we calmed down. Without any hesitation he took his truck keys and left.

That night I wept tears of intense agony. This news was another burden on my fragile emotions and I could not—would not—accept that Shad would go behind our backs and do such a thing. I felt betrayed because while Shad tried to make Dua and her family happy, he was breaking our family apart.

I cried myself to sleep that night, but I woke up in the middle of the night with a panic attack, thinking Shad was still out of the house. I ran to the garage door to see if his truck was there, and it was. I took a deep sigh and thanked God for keeping him safe.

I went to his bedroom just to make sure he was alright. Shad was fast asleep tucked in his comforter. I wanted to put my hand over his head but that would have woken him up. I left his bedroom and went and sat on the couch. Those feelings that I was being punished again returned. I still had no idea why, but the thought wouldn't leave. All I wanted was a happy normal life. Why was turmoil around every corner?

By morning, I felt like I was dying from the inside but mustered up my smile for work. I pretended everything was normal in my life. No one could have guessed how distressed and burnt I was.

I had no energy to argue or fight with Shad. At the end of the day, he was doing whatever he could to make Dua's dad accept him, but the truth was that changing your religion doesn't change your DNA, your identity. By converting, Shad tried to gain acceptance from her dad but regrettably that didn't happen.

For the next few months, the environment of the house was extremely somber. Shad wouldn't come home until late at night and Rowi preferred to eat in her own bedroom or out with friends. The four of us were living under the same roof but there was barely any communication amongst us. My happy family was crumbling into pieces.

Every weekend, Dad would ask if everything was alright, and I had to lie. Dad was lonely and by himself, I didn't want to have him worry about my dysfunctional situation.

Nearly every weekend Rowi would ask if we could go to the mall or grab popcorn and watch a movie at the theatre. I would always decline. I was not in the right frame of mind to do any-thing. My health had undoubtedly been suffering, leading to more frequent migraine and panic attacks, which often landed me in the ER.

It didn't make an inch of a difference to Shad how B and I felt. In fact, I sensed he was proud of his achievement. Many pictures were popping on social media with her family outside the mosque on Eid day. He had totally become a puppet in their hands. My Muslim friends asked me why was Shad at the mosque? My dad had joined Facebook, saw his pictures, and asked me many questions. I didn't lie to my friends, but I lied to my Dad, that Shad met them outside the mosque and took a picture.

When Shad was not at home I snooped in his drawers and found a prayer rug, beads, and books on Islam. I don't know whether he ever used the rug, beads, or even read a page of the book. I never asked him just to avoid conflicts and arguments.

Mind you, don't get me wrong I have absolutely nothing against Muslims or their religion. For thirty-five years I lived in a Muslim country and had some amazing friends. This is my own belief that God could have easily chosen Muslim parents for Shad, but he chose Zoroastrian parents. There has to be a reason for his decision; and I was not going to question God on this one.

* * *

May of 2014 Shad and Dua graduated from Wichita State University. Shad graduated with a bachelor's degree in Criminal Justice. Zarin and Frea had come from Phoenix for his graduation. They had never met Dua and knew nothing regarding the tension in the house.

We were also going to be meeting the family for the first time and that really had me on edge. I had repeatedly asked B and Rowi to be polite and courteous to her family and not create an unnecessary scene and thought the same thing to myself as well. This was Shad's day and if it was going to be ruined, it would not be because of us.

Shad looked very handsome that day with his suit on under his black cap and gown, the yellow cord around his neck, a symbol of excellence.

After the ceremony was over, we met Shad and Dua outside in the packed hallways. She introduced us to her parents and grandparents. Her mom was very warm and welcoming, but the dad met us with a cold handshake and immediately left the hallway. He made it very obvious that he still didn't approve of Shad or the relationship. I could see B's face getting angry, but I kept pressing his arm to let it go.

After Shad and Dua had finished taking their pictures, I nudged Rowi to go and congratulate her. Rowi went up to her with open arms but then my attention was diverted by Dua's mother, just to have a conversation.

From the corner of my eye, I saw B place his arm around Rowi, their faces flustered. Before I could ask if everything was okay, Shad suggested we take a family picture with Dua. In front of everyone, B said "NO" and walked off holding Rowi's hand. My heart sank and I could see the humiliation and hurt on Shad's face, not knowing why his dad had reacted this way.

It was a very awkward moment for me. I was ashamed of how B had behaved. Very politely Zarin, Frea, and I said goodbye to them and started walking toward the parking lot.

B and Rowi were already sitting in the car waiting for us. The minute I sat in the car I said to B, "What in the heck was that. You couldn't be courteous for the sake of your son."

B remained quiet, not saying a single word, or even looking toward me. Thankfully, it was a short drive from WSU to home. When we reached home, B went straight into the bedroom. I was going to follow him and lash out at him, but Rowi told me to pause and listen to what happened.

"Like you suggested I went to congratulate and hug Dua. Instead of hugging back she gave me a hard push and said, "Today I'm special and not you." Dad was the only one who saw everything and that's why he didn't want to take a picture with her.

I felt so uneasy all this craziness taking place in front of Zarin and Frea who had come to celebrate the graduation, which had turned into a soap opera. After thirty minutes, Shad came home huffing and puffing ready to attack his Dad, but before he said anything to B, Rowi told him what had happened. Shad was horrified and confused, as that was not the story he had heard from Dua. He then apologized to Rowi and B for her behavior.

By the grace of God, by dinner time moods had mellowed out and everyone was fine. We came home, had cake and tea, took some more family pictures, and were sitting and chatting when there was a knock at the door. B went to the door to see it was Dua. Without opening the door, B turned to Shad and said, "It's Dua, please ask her to leave."

Shad went up to the door, respected his dad's wishes, talked to her for a while, and came back in.

The rest of the night was good. However, before I went to bed I did my usual check to ensure all the doors were locked. I noticed the garage wasn't and Shad and Dua were talking outside on the back porch swing. I couldn't hear them talking but from the body language it looked like Shad was upset.

After seeing Dua's ill-mannered behavior toward his younger sister, I felt determined that it would be the last straw, that Shad would break up with her once and for all. As most people know, when determination is pitted against determination, only one can win, and sadly that was not me that night. I don't know what sob story Dua gave Shad, but when I asked about everything the next morning, he dismissed it completely.

* * *

That summer, I didn't travel to Karachi. Dad and Fara were disappointed but for once I thought about myself more than anybody else and needed a getaway from Wichita.

I had given too much of my time to other people but now it was high time I gave some time to B, Rowi, and myself. I wanted Shad to go with us for ten days to Phoenix, but he was expecting a phone call to from Border Patrol Texas and hoped for an interview. I'm not sure if that was an excuse or not but it was what Shad offered and he stayed behind, making it a family of three for that trip.

CHAPTER 27

It wasn't just me that needed the Phoenix getaway; we all did. We visited the Mehta's, of course, and also went to Las Vegas. We were about ten miles away from Nevada when we stopped for gas and a bathroom break. When I got out of the car, out of nowhere I was hit by an anxiety attack. I was drained, with zero energy, and had a massive urge to get scurry back home.

I whispered in B's ears that I wanted to go home. B thought maybe the long drive and the heat might be making me feel tired. He bought some Starbucks cold coffee but that didn't make any difference. I quietly sat in the car holding on to B's arms like a little child. With each mile closer to Vegas, my energy dropped, and my anxiety rose.

Before we went to our hotel, Rowi wanted to visit the Gold & Silver Pawn Shop. It is a series filmed on TV where it chronicles the daily activities of a family-owned business. She was hoping to see Rick Harrison, but he was not there. Rowi was as excited as if she was on the show in real time. She was pulling us around as if she was the owner. We spent at least an hour in the shop and then left for the hotel.

Finally, I thought. I needed a rest because I couldn't figure out what was wrong. No answer appeased me.

We were going to meet the Mehta's downstairs at the lobby area at 7 p.m. Rowi was so excited she was dressed and ready to go a half hour early. She kept nudging me to get up and get dressed and I kept saying, "What is the hurry?" I didn't want to get out of bed but at the same time didn't want to ruin our holiday either. Reluctantly, I got dressed and kept saying Dad's magical word, Ahunavar, *please help me God.*

The Strip is lined with upscale casino hotels, which have gambling floors, vast variety of the restaurants and shops, and performance venues for musical shows.

Out of the few casinos we visited, Bellagio was the best. It is a resort, luxury hotel, and casino. One of the most notable features is a lake between the building and the Strip, which houses the Fountains of Bellagio, a large dancing water fountain synchronized to music.

That magical place transported me to calmness, which I will always appreciate. I could have stood there for hours just watching the dancing fountains changing colors as the music's beat shifted.

We also went to Caesar's Palace—a replica of ancient Roman, Greek, and Renaissance periods with beautiful art. The most fascinating thing I saw out there were people pretending to be statues. It was mind blowing how they could stand in one pose for hours without moving. At first, I wouldn't believe they were people, I had to look very closely to see they were not statues. What a difficult job that would be. Hats off to all those people!

After Las Vegas was a trip to Hoover Dam and then Grand Canyon National Park, which was breathtakingly beautiful. As we neared Sedona, I felt as if I was wrapped in a blanket of peace.

At that time I had no idea where we were or anything about Sedona.

When we arrived at the hotel everyone was busy getting their luggage from the van but I kept turning around, trying to see Sedona in the darkness. I said to B, "This place is so tranquil." B brushed me off, saying, "Everyone is sleepy, that's why." That was not what I meant.

Normally I don't sleep well in a new environment but that night I was asleep before my head hit the pillow. The next morning, I woke up early to see the sunrise, but was totally taken aback when I saw the majestic red rocks right in front of our hotel. The formations glowed a brilliant orange and red illuminated by the rising sun.

I put my shoes on and went for a walk. The cool air, the majestic red rocks, and the orange glow of the sun mesmerized me, and I soaked up its special glow as if it were made just for me. I walked for at least two miles, then sat on the bench to appreciate the calm moment.

The reason behind this calmness were the vortexes. A vortex is believed to be a special spot on the earth where energy is either entering into the earth or projecting out of the earth's plane. Sedona is famous for healing, meditation, self-exploration, and yoga retreats. With so much of chaos and turmoil in my life, this magical place provided serenity and tranquility, which I cherished. That day, we didn't take any hikes but just walked around Cathedral Rock and went to Chapel of the Holy Cross.

The rest of the family was outside taking pictures of the scenic view and I was drawn inside the Cathedral. I lit a candle and sat quietly on the bench. I closed my eyes and begged God to make right choices for Shad. If that meant Dua was a part of his life's picture, so be it. I knew it wasn't in my hands but prayed for calmness despite the decision.

I also prayed for Rowi and B to be healthy and safe.

I must have sat there for almost thirty minutes but then I heard a whisper. "Mom, you are on a holiday; can you please come outside."

I turned my head. Rowi and Frea were like two young teenagers. They had their shoes and socks kicked off, jumped into the puddle of water, and splashed water to cool off. They climbed the bare trees and tried to get to the highest branch. It was an awesome time for the two cousins, who were more like sisters, to bond.

I felt Shad's absence. I truly wished for him to be with us. It would have been the first holiday we all took together, and it would have made for precious memories to cherish.

When we returned back to Wichita, we had a good surprise from Shad. We had a long driveway and I always wanted to plant chrysanthemums near the third garage but never found the time and energy to do it. In our absence Shad had removed the white pebbles and made a beautiful flower bed with mums, which would bloom in fall. I was entranced and appreciative with the beautiful surprise.

CHAPTER 28

August of 2014, Rowi was leaving Wichita State University. She wanted to join Kansas State University, mostly known as K-State in Manhattan, Kansas, which was about two hours away from Wichita.

Rowi wanted to be independent and experience University life. But I knew Rowi was not matured and most certainly not yet ready to leave her nest, especially her Daddy, who couldn't live without her either.

I advised her to go the following year but Rowi was adamant. Middle of August we moved all her stuff to a three-bedroom apartment on the campus. She was going to share her apartment with five other girls. Rowi was the first one to move in. She chose the room and bed she wanted.

The size of the apartment was not too bad, but the bedrooms were so tiny even for one person leave alone two.

We were all emotional, especially B about his princess. I just hugged and kissed her a bunch and then gave the usual lectures that moms do when they leave their child on their own. After saying goodbye and waving hundreds of times, I giggled and said, "Oh don't worry, she will be back in two months."

That October, Shad was hired by Derby Police Department. He had to be at the Hutchinson Police Academy for four months, but the nice part was he could come home on the weekends. It seemed all of a sudden, my noisy nest became empty and quiet without my birds. It felt terrible, unusual, and not normal. I had never realized or thought for a minute how much I was going to miss them.

The first few weeks Rowi was happy and excited. But after a month it started to disappear. She had a job at the dining hall serving food and cleaning the kitchen. The hours and schedule were too long and tiring and she was finding it difficult to balance studies, work, do her own laundry, and cook her own meals.

On the weekends, the roommates' boyfriends came over to the apartment (which wasn't "allowed"). They partied all night and left a disastrous apartment for Rowi and her Japanese roommate to clean.

Rowi wasn't used to being in a dirty house and always ended cleaning up the mess. Without asking her permission, they ate her food, used her crockery, and finished her laundry detergent too. She tried to discuss her challenges with her roommates but they paid no attention to her.

One Wednesday that October, Rowi mentioned she was running high fever with pain at her sides. She had seen the nurse who diagnosed her with a kidney infection. The nurse had prescribed her medication, which was making her throw up and feel dizzy. We were constantly on the phone with her but around 7 p.m. her temperature shot up higher.

B and I just couldn't sit at home, so we left for Manhattan to bring her home for the weekend. By the time we picked her up it was late and she went to sleep right away in the back of the car for the two-hour drive home. I stayed home with her the next two days, Thursday and Friday, took her to our wonderful family physician, Dr. Steven Davis, and he prescribed her new medicines.

To clear off her kidney infection I was making her drink lemon water every fifteen minutes and made chicken soup with vegetables. Rowi was always small but she looked thinner and weaker. Her hair had lost its luster too.

She was better by Sunday evening but not happy. She had been very quiet for those few days. I asked if she was packed but she would become teary. I kept asking her what was wrong, but she wouldn't tell me. I asked her if she wasn't feeling well, she could stay for a few more days but she insisted that she was fine.

Later when B came from work, I asked if she had said anything to him. Its unlike Rowi to be so quiet. B looked at me and said, "Yes. I know."

Then B spilled the beans that Rowi was miserable at K-State and didn't want to go back. She was afraid to tell me. Rowi started crying, she was sorry that she disappointed us but the only reason she went to K-State was because she was sick and tired of Dua's behavior and all the constant fights and arguments in the house.

It was painful Rowi didn't open up to me because she thought I would yell at her, give her an "I told you so." But if she would have mentioned to us that she was miserable I would have got her out of K-State sooner.

Rowi's knees were tucked under her chin, tears still streaming down her cheeks. She said, "Ma, why can't Shad see anything beyond her. He is always defending her when he knows she is at fault. It's all in front of him. And now I've made a mistake and left the house to avoid all that, even when I wasn't ready to."

Rowi put her hands in her palms and again started to cry. I gave her a tight long hug. She put her head in my lap and I let her lay there for as long as she wanted and kept caressing her hair. At that moment I reminded her how loved and special she was. Student loans didn't matter, they could be paid like any other loan, but her happiness—that mattered greatly.

However, this didn't fully resolve the problem. After Rowi's return she wasn't her normal perky upbeat self. She was depressed, disappointed with herself. She remained in her room with Max lazing on her bed whilst she created beautiful paintings. That was her solace.

When Shad came home on weekends from the Police Academy, he didn't let her stay in her room but instead dragged her to watch movies, go for their normal drives, and play games at their friend's house.

When Shad would return to the academy, my time with Rowi would start. I used to take her to Kohls, try on the highest heeled shoes with the sexiest dress, and then laugh. We'd send pictures to Shad and B, laughing even harder at our silliness and stupidity.

By December, Rowi was finally feeling better. She was eating healthy food and exercising. She made new friends too. And thanks to my avocado, egg, and oil hair mask, her hair was shiny again. She was getting her sassiness back, which proved she was getting back to normal.

Rowi always loved December and the Christmas season. That Christmas season she decorated the Christmas tree with ornaments, garnished the fireplace with lights, wreaths, stockings, and trinkets, which she made herself.

She placed lights outside the house, on the shrubs and bought presents for each one of us. No doubt the house looked magnificent giving an effect of peace and warmth, however my heart was heavy with thoughts about those children that were neglected and abused.

I didn't want to disappoint Rowi as she had carefully made each ornament, but I explained to her that maybe next year we should not spend so much on us and instead donate food and clothing for an organization. Since Rowi was only twenty, still in her own sweet bubble, she didn't understand what I was trying to teach her. She felt I was angry with her for spending so much of money but that was not my point. I was trying to teach my children that Christmas was not only for presents and decorations but also for giving and showing kindness to others who were less fortunate than them.

Together, my family made a promise that for Christmas 2015, we would each dish out $100, so a total of $400, and we would buy groceries and clothing for the needy.

* * *

January 2015, Rowi was back at WSU and her normal self again. She was doing much better in school, despite her math struggles, but I knew she was trying and not ashamed to ask for extra help from her professors.

She'd pester them until she understood.

Since high school Rowi had been dating a boy. It was a most weird relationship. After school he had joined the Air Force. The only way they had contact with each other was through Skype and text messages, which he was inconsistent with, at best, in answering.

Many times, I'd reminded her that one-sided relationships didn't work. He was not worth her investment.

She'd agree and say it was over. She wasn't going to waste her time any longer. But one apology from him with chocolates, teddy bears, and flowers, would melt her heart and she would be back to square one. Samuel's mom loved Rowi and called her "my brown girl," but unfortunately that kind of love didn't come from him.

Samuel did nothing to demonstrate he deserved a beautiful girl like my Rowena.

*   *   *

February of 2015, Shad graduated from the Police Academy. On his graduation day, upon his insistence, we had invited Dua's family over for dinner. I was extremely nervous, but it went okay. The next day, however, was different. Shad announced that he and Dua were planning to get married May 2016.

I went with the flow, forcing a happy smile. It was so fake. My heart and head were spinning as to how everything would work out financially and emotionally.

Dua had always wanted a Princess wedding and her expectations were way over our budget. I had begged Shad to wait for two years when he was more mature and financially stable. No advice, counseling, or guidance made any difference to him. In fact, it was just creating more ugliness and distance between him and us.

CHAPTER 29

February 18, 2015, Rowi turned 21. She was thrilled to legally have a drink. For her birthday, we took her out to Twin Peaks and the next day she was going to go out with Shad and a few friends to the bar. Shad was supposed to be their chaperone and driver. I was a bit worried and hoping the girls wouldn't get too drunk, except they were back home within an hour. I was surprised to see all of them so early and asked Shad if the girls had not been enjoying themselves.

Shad laughed and said Rowi ordered two margaritas but didn't like either one of them. The bar was too loud, and she wanted to get the heck out of there. I wasn't surprised. Instead of the bar, her friends came to our house, changed into their PJs, made hot chocolate, dipped Oreo cookies in it, and watched movies. B and I chuckled: yes, she was still our little girl!

Dua had been invited to our family dinner but not to the bar with Rowi and her friends. When she found out, she created a scene.

Rowi had tolerated enough and gained some 21-year-old confidence. Rowi said that she had been invited to the family dinner but did not need to be invited everywhere she went, especially with her friends.

Then she added the fuel: you have always bragged that you are a true Muslim and would never drink or go to the bar. So I don't know what your problem is.

I realized that Dua brought three of the four members of our family pain. Rowi had finally had enough.

Up until that point, all three of us tolerated Dua just because of Shad. We just couldn't understand how Shad could love her and want to be her life partner. How would Dua be a supportive wife when all she thought about was herself?

* * *

That March, Thrity masi at age eighty-three went peacefully to heaven. She was depressed and lonely without her husband, Mom, and Khorsh masi.

Shen masi had requested me to vacate her apartment. Since I had helped her move from Parsi Colony to Jamshed Baugh I exactly knew how much paraphernalia she had.

At first, I was going to fly alone to Karachi, but fortunately Emirates tickets were on sale so Rowi came with me. She was most excited to see her grandpa and her friends after five years. Before leaving for Karachi, they had already made their plans for the summer.

By now I had been in the US for eleven years. This was my seventh trip to Karachi. After mom's passing, my trips to Karachi were very depressing. Although I was happy to see Dad, he wasn't my same quirky dad anymore. He had become quiet, impatient, and irritable—cranky.

That year the temperatures in Karachi were record highs and miserable. To make it worse, our Parsi Colony main water got mixed up with the sewage line. Many residents of Parsi Colony were falling sick with stomach issues and eye infections, including Dad, Rowi, and me. In all the years that I had lived in Karachi, I had never experienced anything like that summer. It was awful!

One good thing that came out of this trip was Zarin's visit to Karachi after fifteen years. She came to give me a hand in vacating Thrity masi's house. Until then, Zarin's trips to Karachi had always been in winter when the weather was beautiful.

It took Zarin and I around three days to go through Thrity masi's files and boxes. Our last step would be an estate sale for the remainder of the goods.

We announced via word of mouth that we would start selling items on June 14 at 11 a.m.

Zarin and I were not ready for what happened on June 14 before 11 a.m. As soon as we entered the gates of JB, we saw there was a swarm of women waiting right outside the apartment. It felt like a Black Friday sale where everyone waits outside and gets aggressive to get in the doors to get the best deals first.

The two of us nudged each other and said it was going to be hell, and it was! Everything that we had laid out so neatly and orderly was strewn about within a minute, each one yelling that they found the item first.

Zarin and I had no choice but to throw everyone out. We pushed them out of the house and locked the door, looking at the house in disbelief.

I chuckled. "We will need Roshan aunty's help." The next day we went back with Roshan aunty and sure enough everything was a smooth sail. Everyone in the Zoroastrian Community knows Roshan aunty will not tolerate any ill-mannered behavior from anyone.

It was sad to see masi's belongings leave her house, all the things that Zar and I had seen since we were children. But our main loss was not the things, but our beloved masi who had cared, loved, and spoiled us unconditionally.

Zarin returned to the US and I remained in Karachi with Dad for one more month. This was the first time I was counting days to go back to Wichita. The heat and sewage issues were driving me nuts, Shad's upcoming wedding was giving me anxieties, and to top everything, my dad was driving me insane.

Dad was taking out his frustrations and anger out on me. He said nasty things to me when no one was around and I tried to overlook them. This wasn't always possible.

One evening a few neighbors came to visit Dad. I had just come home from running errands and was hot and sweaty, preferring not to go outside to greet them. But those ladies asked about me. Before I had the chance to at least wash my face and change clothes, I heard Dad's ugly words. "She must be sleeping or reading, that's all she does." I held my chin high, ignored what Dad had just said, and greeted the ladies very politely. One of the ladies said to Dad, "Ya right, we see her all the time running around in this heat." That neighbor had no idea how good that made me feel.

Many times, the neighbors had seen and waved to me, whilst I was walking toward the main road to catch a rickshaw.

Then after a few days, Dad's car wasn't working. It was a 1985 Suzuki car, which had been used for years for his business and family. I suggested to Dad that since he doesn't drive anymore, he should sell the car and use the money to ease his burdens.

Something got into that man, and he told me that B used to use the car and ever since then it gave him trouble. Oh no. Those words flipped my patience switch.

I said, "Dad, B has not touched your car in over eleven years. It's an old car, which you used to carry paint drums, tools, planks, everything that you needed for your business. Why accuse one person; it's wear and tear. The man you are accusing of spoiling your car has always found a way to pay for my tickets to Karachi and send you money whenever possible. B will be extremely annoyed with me that I said this to you, but it hasn't been easy for us either to make all these trips.

"I have spent many of my summer holidays here in this scorching heat. The same amount of money I could have used to go on a holiday within the US with my family. But instead, I have been coming here to take care of you and this is what I have to hear."

I think the last sentence really got him as he became very quiet after that. With my voice choking, I continued that I was sorry for not being as bright and clever as Fara. I shared that over the years he caused me pain many times. I had remained quiet because he was my dad, I loved him, and didn't want to hurt his feelings. I concluded with, "I can't take this anymore. Just accept me for who I am and not for who I am not."

There, I'd said my peace.

For two or three days there was not much of a conversation between Dad and me. We talked only if we had to. We both were in our own world of thoughts. I was happy to hear Rowi talk nonstop and give all the juicy Zoroastrian gossip to us and to not pretend to make a conversation. In the evenings when Rowi was out with friends, Dad would spend time outside with neighbors or watch National Geographic. I wasn't interested in either but did whatever he wanted to do. I didn't want to isolate him from me, as I knew the days were getting closer for us to leave.

A few days before I was leaving for US, Dad gave me a check of Rupees One lakh, which was equivalent to $1500. Dad wanted Shad to buy a suit as a wedding present from him. I refused to take money from him, as that was a lot of money for Dad. He insisted that it would make him happy. As much as I tried to reason with him to keep that money, he wouldn't listen but instead he kept saying, "I only have a little time left, what will I do with the money?"

My heart was so heavy that tears started to roll down my cheeks. I placed my hands over his old, wrinkled hands and said, "Dad, please don't talk like that, Fara and I still need you around."

He looked at me and gave me a smile but deep beneath his smile was grief, pain, and loneliness. I got up from the couch next to him, sat on the floor and placed my head in his lap, just as I had Mom's that one day. In silence, he stroked my hair and I cried quietly.

To this day, I do not know why my dad said things that were so hurtful. I wish he would have just seen the real me inside out.

That summer it was difficult to leave Dad. Rowi and I returned back to US at the end of July. B and Shad picked us up from Dallas Fort Worth International the next morning. That night in the hotel I must have stood in the shower for at least fifteen minutes letting water run over every bit of my body. I wanted all the dirty, foul, unclean microorganism, pathogens to get off me. I must have shampooed and washed my body at least thrice, to feel absolutely clean and fresh. I have never once in my entire life valued clean water, fresh washed clothes, and a soft towel so much. It was truly a lesson learnt, to value and thank God for the smallest blessings in our lives.

CHAPTER 30

The wedding invitations were printed and except for the invites and our saris there was nothing ready for the wedding. At the end of August, I asked Shad about wedding details and all he said was, "Oh, don't worry; everything is being taken care of." Feeling unsatisfied, I went to Dua. She gave the same nonchalant answers.

Their answers were not what I was looking for. He was my son and as much as I was against this marriage, I wanted to be involved in the planning too. Frustrated, I called Dua's mom on August 30th. I remember it precisely. When I complained to her mom about not knowing anything regarding the wedding, she promised she would find out more details and we could meet together and finalize everything.

A month later, still no phone call from her. Out of frustration I gave the box of invitations to Shad. Since no one was interested to include us in the wedding preparations then it was better he wrote the invitations by himself and planned the whole event with her family.

September of 2015, Muslims were celebrating Eid. For B, Rowi, and I it was just another normal working day.

B called me at noon and said Shad was just visiting him at Dillon's. Dua's Dad was going to invite us for dinner that night at Texas Roadhouse. B chuckled that it was already noon, and it would be interesting to see how long it took. When I got home hours later, it was Shad inviting us to dinner, not her dad.

I asked him why he was doing the invite when Dua's dad had the whole day to call. I said, "Dad and I are not going any-where; you can go to their family dinner." Shad raising his voice at me said, "Jeez, Mom, why do you make a big deal out of everything?" That was it, my turning point. I became infuriated with him.

I started yelling at Shad that he wasn't understanding my point. All I was trying to tell him that if Dua's father was invit-ing us then he should have called Dad or I and not asked you to convey the message. I said Shad I'm sorry but we are not going to this dinner.

The next thing that came out of Shad's mouth was unbeliev-able and devastating. He screamed, "MOM, SCREW YOU!"

I looked at Shad in disbelief. His words said it all about what he was thinking at that moment. I stared at him for a few seconds, wondering if that had really happened or it was my imagination.

I asked him what he said again. "Screw you," he repeated.

I raised my hand to slap him across his face, but he moved away. It didn't take long for me to get hysterical and start flailing at him and hitting him wherever my hands could connect. Out of anger and contempt I said, "I wish you would have died the day you were born." I went to my bedroom and locked the door. My heart was racing as if I had run a marathon. I still couldn't believe what I had just heard, especially for a man who would never accept and respect Shad or us from his heart, but I was no better. What came out of my mouth was unacceptable and horrifying.

Behind the door I could hear Rowi shrieking at Shad, asking him to get out of the house until things cooled down, but Shad didn't leave.

Again, I heard Rowi screaming, "Enough is enough.

Get out of the house and do whatever the hell you want."

Then Rowi started to cry and that's when I left the bedroom. At that moment, B came home. At first, he couldn't understand what was going on because Rowi and Shad were trying to talk at the same time. B had to yell at both of them to be quiet and then he heard the whole story from Rowi.

B gave Shad a frustrated look and said, "I hope the people that you are fighting for and abusing your mother are worth it."

The atmosphere of the house became extremely quiet and somber. Rowi locked herself in her room, Shad had left the house to catch some fresh air, and I was cuddled in my blanket.

When Shad returned, he apologized for his behavior and was extremely sorry for what he had said earlier. Then he said what I didn't want to hear; he was moving out of the house.

Before I could say anything or stop him, B said to Shad that he was an adult and could make his own decisions. If that was what he wanted to do, then he should.

After Shad left the room, I was upset with B for saying that to him, not because B was wrong but because I didn't want him to be right. It was part of my cultural upbringing and how children usually progressed to their next stage but it was so hard. Shad didn't come to ask permission if he could leave, he was just informing us that he was moving out. I was absolutely devastated by another impulsive decision. Yes, I was angry and hurt at what had happened, and I apologized for my behavior too, as it was wrong. I begged him not to move out, but he did. After a week, Shad moved into a decent sized one-bedroom apartment. He'd live there for six months and after May Dua and he would move into a two-bedroom apartment.

When he was in the process of moving out, Shad asked B if he wanted his truck back. B mentioned, no you can keep it and take the garage opener with you. It's your house, you can come whenever you want.

As much as I hated the idea of Shad moving, I was elated to know I wouldn't have to see Dua or her siblings.

I had external peace after that but the same was not true for my internal peace. For a few weeks, Shad and I didn't talk about Dua or the wedding. I hoped it was that he was having second thoughts but that was a dream, not reality. Since no one was interested to tell me anything I kept out of it and let them manage the whole wedding.

After a few weeks Shad asked if I wanted to go and check out the venue. I honestly didn't want to go wanted to calm the waters and make him happy.

Whilst Shad was showing me around, Dua and her siblings were there giving instructions to Shad regarding decoration. Dua's mom never apologized for not calling, but casually mentioned about the catering of a Mehendi ceremony. I was confused and clueless. From my expression she said with a chuckle that Dua must have forgotten to inform you. Her dad insists on having a Mehendi ceremony, as its important in our culture.

A Mehendi ceremony takes place two or three days before the wedding. The women in the family along with close friends, gather together while the bride has elaborate henna designs applied to her hands and feet. This goes along with lots of food, music, and dance. I didn't ask one single question regarding the ceremony. I smiled said thank you for the invitation my whole family will be there:

"Not my circus, not my monkeys."

* * *

November of 2015 came extremely fast and it was already Thanksgiving. I was surprised Shad didn't go to Dua's grandma's house for their usual Thanksgiving feast but came home.

Shad and Rowi wanted a Thanksgiving dinner but not the usual turkey or green beans casserole. They liked steaks with the typical Pakistani spices, granny style mashed potato—meaning from scratch—and dinner rolls with butter.

Rowi always grumbled and made a fuss that there was no dessert but could barely finish her dinner. She would want ten dishes on the table but couldn't even eat half of what she had taken. But instead of having a heavy dessert, we would always have "After Eight" chocolates, just something light and sweet.

After dinner, Shad and Rowi decorated the Christmas tree, with their usual sibling bickering about which ornament goes where, at the same time trying to chase Max away as he also wanted to be a part of the fun.

That year we didn't buy any Christmas gifts for each other or new ornaments, just like I'd requested the previous Christmas. We had enough from last year, we most certainly didn't need anymore.

Rowi found Wichita Children's Home, which is a non-profit organization that offers emergency, temporary, and residential care for children in the community. They fulfil their needs and ensure the safety of these precious neglected and abused children. I wish we could have bought much more but $400 is all we could afford. The cart was full of clothes, food, and games.

We did the best we could and promised that we would continue giving every year.

When Rowi and I went to deliver all the items, coincidentally Rowi was wearing her WSU shocker hoodie. The lady at the reception asked Rowi what was her degree in? Rowi said proudly, I am a junior in psychology and plan to do my Masters in Teen Psychology. The lady started asking more questions to Rowi and inquired if she was interested in working at WCH. Rowi became their youngest part time faculty member in January 2016.

* * *

After Christmas, Rowi ignored B's and my wishes and went to visit her boyfriend in Colorado at the Air Force base. We didn't want her to leave but she needed answers from that boy once and for all.

I was a nervous wreck for a week. I called her several times in a day just to make sure she was doing well. She sounded unhappy, which made me edgier.

My main concern was her safety, but I could hear other voices over the phone so at least that was a bit of a relief. Finally, she came home, drained and melancholic. From her face it seemed as if she had been crying all the way to Wichita. I asked if everything was okay, she immediately teared up and said, "Mom, he doesn't love me the way I love him. He wasn't really happy to see me, and we barely spent time together. We went out once because I insisted."

I kept my "I told you so" to myself and worked on soothing her heart. I suggested to Rowi to bid him farewell and close that chapter of her life forever. Some things just were not meant to be.

CHAPTER 31

Let's start by me saying that to this day I wish I could erase 2016 from my life.

Though it had been three months since Shad had moved out he still came home to check on Rowi, mostly. Every time they would leave for their little sibling time, I could hear them bickering about who was paying. Each said the other one was. I never bothered to ask who paid for who.

The wedding was nearing and there was little conversation about it. All I knew at this point they were having a civil marriage, and I was paying for the catering of the wedding.

I had begun writing invitations, not waiting on Shad, and getting organized for family members staying with us. I was more ready for the family then I was for the wedding. I still had no idea regarding the flower arrangements, wedding cake, or what Rowi and I were wearing at the Mehendi ceremony. I'd moved past even attempting to get answers to those questions.

I was surprised when Shad asked if I wanted to have any Zoroastrian ceremonies? My very prompt reply was "NO."

* * *

Working at the Children's Home provided a 180 degree turn in Rowi's life. She started taking more interest in her studies and became more involved in improving the lives of the neglected teenage girls. Since there was not much age difference between them, she became their sister, friend, and mentor. The days she was off, she would tell us stories of how she didn't appreciate some of the other faculty members mistreating these girls. Some days she would have a sparkle in her eye and laugh that the faculty member from the boy's side thought she was one of the girls and asked her why she was outside. She would continue with a smile that she showed him her faculty card and he was still in disbelief. He kept asking how it was possible because she looked twelve.

Over the years, I had also heard the name of Dane Owens a lot. He was also a student at Wichita State working at the same office as Shad and Dua.

I clearly remember the day Dane started to become a problem. It was a Friday and Rowi was off from work.

Dane asked Rowi if she was interested to get dinner and movie. Rowi agreed to go but couldn't get ahold of him as late as 6:00 p.m.

Finally, at 8:00 p.m. Rowi called his house to make sure nothing had happened to him. Rowi found out that he had been out with his friends. Rowi was really confused, as she didn't understand why he asked her if he had plans to hang out with friends. Rowi was irritated, said he was weird, then went on to do something else.

Since I had only heard very good things about Dane I didn't give it another thought. I also just thought boys will be boys and don't always realize how their oversights can be hurtful to someone else.

As time passed by, I felt that Rowi and Dane had a soft corner for each other. But in my opinion, I also felt Rowi was on a rebound.

* * *

Very soon it was April and yet I only knew from Shad were the two venues of the ceremonies and the catering. Dua's family were organizing the whole wedding as to what she wanted. Shad was just a groom who just had to show up with his family.

According to Dua it was her Princess wedding, whatever that meant exactly. For the sake of our child, we went along with it with as much respect for Dua and her family as we could muster.

Rowi was planning to give Shad an album of Shad and Dua's pictures from Shutterfly. She asked Shad what color he would like for the background? As we all know boys are so oblivious to all these color combinations, he expressed that any color that she chooses would be great.

One day Rowi and I were in the parking lot of Bed Bath and Beyond when her cell rang. It was Dua on the phone. She was raging in anger as to why she was not consulted for the background coloring of the album.

Without a beat, Rowi shot back at her, shaking her head, and pointing her finger. "This gift is from a sister to her brother. You just happen to be in the pictures. I asked Shad about the colors, and he asked me to put in any color I wanted. My brother is so stupid to even ask you."

I could hear Dua shouting that this color doesn't match with her wedding theme.

Rowi angrily responded to Dua that she wasn't making any sense at all and hung up on her. Then we looked at each other in disbelief. What did the Shutterfly album have to do with the wedding color theme?

The month of May should have brought happiness and excitement in our house but I was a nervous wreck. My family members were asking too many questions of me, many for which I had no answers.

For months, Shad was insistent that they were having a civil ceremony, not a Nikah ceremony. B and I knew in our hearts that would never happen. Dua's dad was a Muslim who would never approve of this marriage without the very important ceremony.

I wanted to believe Shad but deep inside of me I knew he was lying. The only good thing that I hoped would come out of the wedding was a family reunion where I could see loved ones and meet new people from my family that I had yet to meet.

The events came. We made it through the Mehendi ceremony, but I felt my intense anxieties taking over. I had this horrible nudge that this was going to be his biggest mistake of his life.

I drifted off and woke up to the onset of an anxiety attack. I went outside to try and ground myself. I watched the beautiful colors of the sky, but my mind wandered to the day Shad had fought with me, abused me, and moved out. I tried to push it out of my mind but the feeling was persistent and strong. I was still hurting and in pain thinking of all the things he had done behind our backs, all to please them without any regard about how it had broken our hearts. But he was my sweet little boy and no matter what he did, I loved him.

169

The morning was extremely busy with family over for breakfast. After that all the ladies were getting ready with showers, as everyone had hair appointments. A week before the wedding, Shad had emptied the apartment, shifted his stuff to the new one but wasn't staying there. He had come home until his wedding. Shad was all dressed up in a nice shirt and dressed pants. I asked him where was he going that early?

Shad replied halfheartedly that he had to take care of a few things at the venue. I asked if I could make some breakfast for him but except for tea he declined everything. Very unusual for Shad to refuse a good breakfast. I chalked it up to nerves…which made sense, as evidenced by me.

Rowi looked stunning in her royal blue colored saree with silver sequins. The border of the saree was embroidered in gold flowers with a black background. For jewelry she had a gold choker chain and on her thin arms she had blue and gold matching bracelets. Her long hair was curled but pinned from the sides. This was the first time she had worn a saree and I must admit she walked and danced very graciously in it.

Shad was supposed to leave with his best man Kyle at 3:30 p.m. but at 3:45 p.m. he was still in his bedroom.

The photographer wanted to take pictures of Shad and Dua before the guests arrived.

I rushed down to see what was going on and why he hadn't left. Shad was sitting on the end of his bed in his T shirt and shorts. He was in his own world, just staring into space. The look on his face was sorrowful. I didn't ask him what was wrong, but I gently said, "You know you don't have to do this if it doesn't feel right. You still have time."

At first, he didn't answer but then he said, "Mom! Family have come from so far; I can't do this to them." I sat on the bed with him and explained that family wasn't important at this time but his whole entire life depended on his decision. I placed my hand over his head and said whatever you decide I will support you. Then I left.

When Shad came upstairs, he didn't look like a groom. His white shirt was not tucked neatly, his gray tie was hanging loose, shoes were untied, belt and suit jacket in his hand.

Kyle remarked, "Dude! Seriously, are you going like this?" Without uttering another word, Shad went and sat in Kyle's truck.

The rest of the family reached the venue at the given time, which was 6 p.m. Dua's siblings were dressed in beautiful shalwar kameez and were handing flower pins to us. Then we were escorted to our tables like passengers on an aircraft.

I will say the venue was very tastefully decorated.

On the stage there were two flower arrangements with white and pink flowers with a blue tablecloth, which were on each side of the stage. Strings of lights hung from one side of the room to the other, which gave a very sweet effect to the venue.

Dua was waiting in the bridal room for the priest to come. Until then, everyone was busy clicking pictures with Shad and I was introducing my Wichita Montessori friends to my whole family. The Maulvi was supposed to come at 7:00 p.m. but there was a miscommunication between the priest and her mom. He showed up a half hour late. I didn't care, the later the better.

In a short while Dua entered with her parents and siblings. She looked very pretty with an off-white sequins shalwar kameez with high heels. Her head was covered with a long dupatta. Shad was looking very handsome too.

Thankfully he had straightened himself up, his tie was well made, and his shirt was tucked in neatly. The maulvi gave a short speech and then had them sign the papers. Now officially they were married.

But whatever that I was feeling deep down inside I didn't let it come out. After they signed the papers, I kissed and congratulated them both and kissed Dua again on her forehead, welcoming her to our family. I put my hand on her head and with genuine feelings said "God bless" to her. B and I both went up to her family, congratulated and hugged each one of them. None of them came to our side of the family and congratulated us, but that was fine.

Though this was a mixed marriage, the ceremony and style were of a typical Muslim wedding. After they signed the papers, Shad and Dua were seated on a couch at the stage taking pictures with everyone. After Dua's family had finished with their photographs, I asked Shad if we could have a photograph of the two sisters' families.

Before Shad could answer, Dua said very rudely, "For pictures you will have to ask Julie, as she is the one who is coordinating with the photographer." I looked at her in disbelief. I looked at Shad and said, "WOW!" I very politely added, "It's okay, I changed my mind."

I was walking down the stage when Shad held my hand and pleaded to stay on stage while he brought the others.

But I couldn't hold on to my tears anymore. I let go of Shad's hand and walked off the stage. Seeing my face, B was conscious that something had gone wrong, but he didn't know what had happened. B gave a nudge to Shad to leave and go back to the stage. Very reluctantly he left but his face and body language were very clear that he was perturbed.

After a few minutes Shad came back to call us for the pictures but I again declined. I know it sounds terrible, but I was so wounded. Words like crushed, hurt, dismayed don't do justice to how I felt at that time.

I had to pull myself together because my emotions were evident. I had to push them—and the tears—aside and go mingle with my friends, distract myself.

After the photographs were done Shad and Dua had their first dance as Mr. & Mrs. After their dance, the music changed, and the young crowd joined in. Very shortly later dinner was served. Dinner was catered from Passage to India. After dinner there was the cake cutting ceremony.

After the cake cutting ceremony, finally Shad got a chance to mingle with his friends and family. All his young cousins, especially the girls, dragged him back to the dance floor.

Shad was on the floor with seven-year-old Aleezay in his hands. Aleezay is my very dear friends Sidra and Moazzam's daughter. They had come especially from California for the wedding. Shad and Aleezay were joined by Rowi and all the cousins. Undoubtedly, they were all having a fantastic time, when suddenly the colorful disco lights disappeared, and a sad song started to play.

At first, we thought it was a mistake by the disc jockey but then we saw that Dua's family was crowded around her with the Quran over her head. Nobody from their family informed us that the bride and groom were about to leave. Even Shad was surprised, given the expression on his face.

Fara whispered to me, "Why do they have such a sad crying song?" My reply: "No idea."

The song, chosen for her bridal exit, was from the Bollywood movie Baabul. All the guests who were familiar with the movie were surprised with her choice. In the movie this song is played when the father-in-law is trying to console his young, widowed daughter-in-law to start living her life again. This song didn't make any sense. Then again, none of this made sense to me.

173

After Shad and Dua left, many guests also started leaving. We had to leave the venue by 11:00 p.m. so we began to clean up the tables.

By now, you may be thinking I was overly protective of my children and trying to dictate their lives but neither assumption is true. I don't understand how and why I have known certain things either by catching a glimpse or via a thought; however, when I've shared those thoughts as a cautionary tale I've received that irritating, yet typical reaction of "WHATEVER."

This is one of those moments.

Most of the guests had left only family members and very close friends stayed to help clean up. I noticed a boy fluttering around Rowi. No doubt he was helping her to pick up the flower arrangements. I had never seen him before and thought he must be Dua's guest. But I noticed they seemed to know each other. They were very comfortable in each other's presence, enjoying the other's company. I watched quietly from a distance wondering who he was.

Rowi and I met glances and she walked with him and introduced me to him. "Mom, meet Dane." A cold chill ran down my neck all the way to my spine. I couldn't believe this was Dane. He was definitely not the image I had in my mind. I had heard this name a lot in a very positive manner, but my gut instinct didn't react that way. After exchanging handshakes and a few pleasantries, he left with his parents.

I pulled Rowi by her arm into a corner and asked her to stay the heck away from him. He was nothing but EVIL. Those are extremely heavy words to say about someone whom I didn't even know but that's exactly how I felt and I was blunt in expressing it.

After the wedding, everyone went to their hotel, changed from suits and sarees, and came back for tea and coffee. Fara, Zar, and I were whipping coffee when Zarin asked if I knew anything about Shad and Dua's morning wedding. My heart sank and probably missed many beats. I immediately knew this is where he went in the morning all dressed up.

Since Zarin used to be an audiology professor at WSU she knew someone who worked with Shad and Dua. When he met Zarin at the wedding he asked why Shad's family was not present at the mosque for the morning wedding?

Zarin asked him what morning wedding?

The gentleman looked surprised and said the one at the mosque. I was invited for a morning wedding, but I didn't see anyone from Shad's family.

I didn't want to create a scene, but I cried—again. It was so pitiful and embarrassing. B and I had asked him a number of times if there was a Muslim Nikah wedding and every time he had denied there was. Another lie. When was this going to end?

Back to Zar's question, I admitted we knew nothing about it. If he didn't have the decency and love for his parents, what could I do? It was his life; he had dug a hole for himself and he had to live in it. As for me, I was sick of the constant battle.

In spite of so many people in my house, I had to leave the guests and hide in the bathroom for a while. Deep down in my heart I had always known Shad's wedding would be a mess but didn't know it would be miserably painful.

CHAPTER 32

When you feel overwhelmed with problems what is one more. Rowi wanted a German Shepherd. Though B and I love dogs, especially German Shepherds, we weren't so sure Max would like to share his domain.

We were not too keen on getting another dog but agreed to visit the breeders close to Wichita. None of them really impressed us. Then B came across a breeder in Oklahoma, who used to breed and train German Shepherds for the Oklahoma Police Department. This breeder had one dog left—a female—and she was gorgeous. We decided to give Rowi a surprise, so whilst she was at WSU summer school, B and I drove two hours to Perry, Oklahoma, and brought the puppy home.

Rowi walked in the house without a clue that a new friend was waiting for her. When she saw the puppy she started to scream and couldn't stop. She picked up that sweet puppy and began to hug and kiss it profusely. Then we all came up with a name— Sasha.

Sasha was truly gorgeous. Black and brown fur, thick paws, big brown eyes, and typical German Shepherd big ears.

My poor sweet Max was watching all the excitement from a corner of the room. His face was sad and jealous, as he had been the king of the house and was not ready to share his house or family with this new puppy. I wish I would have captured Max's sad face, whilst the others were entertaining Sasha. I placed Max on my lap, comforting and kissed his forehead, assuring him that he would always be my favorite.

Then what happens to a lot of parents who buy a dog for their child happened to B and I. Sasha became our responsibility. It was like having a two-year-old in the house. She barked and scratched her kennel all night, we had no choice but to put her on our bed. Very conveniently Sasha slept with her head on B's stomach and legs toward me, barely giving me any space to sleep. Sasha was happy and excited to see all of us, but her favorite was B. Once B got home, she couldn't care less about anyone else.

* * *

End August of 2016, Rowi announced that she and Dane had started dating. My heart started pounding. I tried to reason with her, but she brushed me off.

A few weeks later, end September during dinner B and I noticed that Rowi's mind was adrift, we asked if everything was alright. We weren't prepared for her answer.

Everything came out, including the tears. Rowi shared: "Dane is having shoulder surgery at the end of the month in Manhattan. The next day his mother is going to drive him to their house. His parents are going out of town, and he has asked me to stay at his house to help him out. I don't want to go but he is insisting."

I blurted out my first gut response. "OH HELL TO THE NO!"

However, we could tell there was more to it than just a shoulder surgery. Rowi placed her fork down and admitted that she had made a mistake. Rowi went on that Dane was fun when they were friends but ever since they had been dating, he had become weird. He had talked about marriage and a family too, ignoring what Rowi had said that it hadn't even been a year since she'd broken up with her high school romance. She had said that she wanted to take it slow, finish her education, and get a job. Then she could think about marriage.

At first, he agreed to everything that she said but it didn't last long. When they started dating there were several things she didn't know but now she did, and they freaked her out.

At this point, B and I were equally troubled and totally distressed. What I had been telling her was not my imagination. B and I both begged Rowi to end it as soon as possible. It wasn't worth spending even a day with a man who freaked you out.

Rowi said he was a good and caring friend that she'd mistaken as someone who could be more than that. The next day Rowi broke off her relationship with him and he didn't take it well. That night at dinner Dane kept texting. B and I were united in our requests for her to ignore and block his number. However, even though she didn't receive messages that didn't mean Dane was out of the picture. There was some kind of fear, panic a fright that something tragic is going to happen.

I couldn't sleep that night. In the middle of the night, I went into Rowi's bedroom in the basement, but she was fast asleep. I knew I wouldn't get a chance to talk to her in the morning, so I texted her at 2:56 a.m., pouring out my heart and my worries about the situation. Rowi could read it when she woke up.

"Lola" I said pleadingly to my girl, "last night I couldn't sleep well. I am not getting good vibes or feelings about Dane but now I feel that he could physically hurt you. It's weird because I didn't get this kind of vibe before. Please! Think a trillion times before you decide anything. I could see it in your eyes yesterday that you didn't want to do this."

Rowi answered in the morning. "I don't think I'm going to do it, Mom. If I didn't have a reason to leave, I wouldn't have. I left for a reason why go back?"

"Oh God thank you. But I'm still worried about him hurting you."

Rowi had made it quite clear to Dane, she didn't want anything to do with him anymore, but he kept on harassing her through text messages and Facebook. When all communication was blocked, he still didn't stop. He found other ways to get his message through to her. By this time, Rowi was worried and irritated. Shad finally stepped in and told Dane to leave Rowi alone. Dane promised that he would stop and that he was sorry.

CHAPTER 33

Friday, September 30th, 2016, was a perfect day for a BBQ outside. B and Shad went to get all the groceries, marinated chicken for tikkas and ground beef for kebabs, and got beer and chips. Everything was ready we were just waiting for Rowi to get home from work.

B and Shad were talking about work, while I was sitting quietly in my own thoughts. After a while, Dua asked if I was okay?

I vented out to her regarding Dane. I acknowledged that he said he'd leave Rowi alone, but I didn't believe it. It was repulsive to say but I kept repeating that I thought Dane might hurt my daughter, but no one believed me.

I begged Shad to file a police report or have a restraining order against him but he felt the matter was resolved. Dua agreed with Shad. They all thought I was overreacting.

In spite of my nervousness, we did have a lovely BBQ. The next day Shad took a day off and insisted that the three of us go watch the movie "Sully" at The Warren 21 Theatre.

To watch a movie at Warren 21 Theatre you have to be over 21 to enjoy the experience because you can have food and alcohol.

We were just five minutes from home when Rowi said she had forgotten her driver's license, which they would require to see if she was over 21. Shad very confidently assured her that he was a cop and that they would take his word. Rowi and I thought we were close enough to home to turn around. Stubborn Shad just boasted that it wouldn't be a problem. Rowi and I chuckled and decided to roll with it.

When we asked at the box office for three tickets to Warren 21, the lady only asked for Rowi's ID. Rowi said she had forgotten her wallet at home and didn't have her ID, but she was over 21.

Shad intervened, "I am a cop."

Before Shad could continue the lady said to Shad that he may be a cop but she still needed her ID.

Rowi and I burst out laughing. It was just too funny not to laugh. Poor Shad's face was priceless and he felt insulted. If only he would have listened to us, we would have had the chance to watch the movie at Warren 21.

* * *

Monday, October 3, 2016, started like any usual morning getting ready to go to work. Before leaving, B made Rowi's cold coffee and bagel with cream cheese. I went to her bedroom in the basement, woke her up, kissed her forehead, said I love you, and left.

Since the week of October 3, I was off from ASP so Rowi would typically have picked me up at 3:15 p.m. from school, taken me home, and then left for the Children's Home.

It was around 1:30 p.m. when B nervously asked if I had heard anything from Rowi, her cell was going directly to voicemail. I tried to call her too, and then we even had Shad try. All our calls were declined. I started to panic the way a mother does when she thinks she should hear from her child but does not. I couldn't do anything since I was without a car. I kept trying every five minutes but no luck.

B was also in a panic and by 3:30 p.m. there was still no sign of her and my coworker Jennifer offered to take me home. Whilst we were still on our way, B must have called at least seven to eight times asking if I was home. Then he said I can't wait any longer; I'm also leaving and coming home. When we reached up to the driveway nothing looked out of the ordinary. The garage door was closed. I punched in the keypad and as the door went up, I saw Rowi's car parked to the left of the garage where she normally parks.

Since Jennifer's daughter was also in the car, she remained in the driveway with her. Our garage door leads directly into the kitchen, which leads to our dining area.

As I swung open the kitchen door, my heart dropped and I was instantly shocked, in utter disbelief as my world immediately spun out of control. My precious sweet, gorgeous Rowi was lying on the floor with blood gushing from her head. My worst fears had come crashing down on me. Oh, how I wished I had been overly dramatic and wrong.

Rowi was hurt and laying in front of me, unconscious in a pool of blood. Max and Sasha sat beside her.

I screamed and yelled. "Rowi, Rowi, what happened?" I was shaking her to answer but there was no response.

Jennifer heard me shouting hysterically and came near the garage door. I ran to her, howling. "Call 911, call 911. She is bleeding from her head, I don't know what has happened!"

Whilst Jennifer was talking to 911 dispatcher, I ran back to Rowi. I was delirious and desperate to get through to my unresponsive child. "Did Dane hit you?" I looked and noticed a screwdriver on the dining table. I kept screaming and shouting at her, "Did Dane hurt you?" But no response. I had no problem going right to the conclusion it was Dane. That was the only conclusion that was logical—nothing made sense to me though.

B Facetimed me and asked if I found her. It was crazy that I answered but I screamed to him through gasping convulsions of tears. "Rowi is bleeding, she is not answering. Come quick!"

I cradled Rowi and tried to call Shad, but he didn't answer. So, I Facetimed him too. He finally answered. "Rowi is bleeding and not responsive." That was all I could say.

The sounds of sirens came blaring up the street. B walked into the house.

I could not process what was happening. I felt sick to my stomach and ran to the bathroom.

Suddenly there was a loud bang on the bathroom door. It was the Wichita police officer asking me to come out. I cried that I was sick and using the bathroom, but he still kept pounding on the door. I yelled back and told him he'd have to open the damn door...but he didn't. He waited at the door until I had finished and then escorted me outside. I begged the officer to let me go near Rowi, but he wouldn't let me go anywhere near her.

The police officer's very first question, "Does she have a boyfriend? Do you suspect anyone?"

Without a trace of hesitation I said, "Rowena just broke off with her boyfriend a few days ago. His name is Dane Owens, but I don't know his address."

Just in time, Dua showed up and gave all the information to the police officer.

There were at least twenty-five officers and detectives on my property. Few outside placing the yellow crime scene tape around the perimeter of the house. I felt as if I was watching a Netflix movie or was in a scary dream. How could this possibly be happening to us?

The officer who had escorted me out asked me several questions and then escorted B, Dua, and myself in three different police cars. B became very hysterical, begging the police officers to let us go with Rowi, but they wouldn't allow us to get out of the police car, let alone go with Rowi.

Whilst we were still waiting in the police car, Rowi was swept away in a speeding EMS. I was frantically pleading the officer to take me to the hospital. The police officer was a woman and very gently and politely made me understand that they have to take some necessary measures and couldn't take me to the hospital. She put her hand on my shaking knees and explained that all three of you will have to go to Wichita Downtown Police Station and will be interrogated in different rooms by detectives.

It had been more than an hour I had been sitting in the police car. I just couldn't sit anymore. I requested if I could lie down at the back seat. Since I couldn't do anything, I just kept praying and begging God to keep my Rowi safe in his arms.

After an agonizing hour later, we headed to the police station. Since it was after office hours there were only a few people on that floor. I was escorted in a small room with just a table and two chairs. My hands and knees couldn't stop shaking. I was so nervous and worried I started to cry.

Homicide Detective Schomaker was very respectful. He asked if I needed water or something to eat. I only asked for water and tissues but nothing else.

The interrogation started at 6:08 p.m. Before he started with the questions he apologized and said that he knew I wanted to be with my daughter but they needed to know what I had seen— what had happened to her.

Detective Schomaker interrogated me for two long agonizing hours. At that time, I was very restless and irritated but now I understand he was only doing his job. His questions started from my name, address, place of employment how many years we have been in Wichita. Our relationship with Rowi. When he asked me questions regarding Rowi and Dane, I gave the same answer I gave to the other detective that I am 100% sure it is Dane who has done something to her. I also showed him my text to Rowi where I had written that I have a feeling he is going to hurt you. I told Detective Schomaker that I begged my daughter to stay away from him but unfortunately, she didn't take my words seriously. I kept interrupting him, asking if he knew anything regarding Rowi but very politely he always declined.

After two hours he apologized for keeping me so long and said the police officer would drive me to the hospital. By the time I went to Westley Medical Center it was nearly 8:30 p.m. I was so nervous and jittery, not knowing what to expect. But just to comfort myself, I kept saying he probably hit her with the screwdriver but not hard enough for any long-term damage. She would be fine.

Reality was about to change my life forever. The officer escorted me to the seventh floor where they had their ICU units. As the elevator door opened there were several police officer's standing in the hallway. Most of them were from Derby and a few from Wichita.

As I entered the unit, Rowi was fast asleep like Sleeping Beauty. Her head was covered in a thick warm fuzzy blanket, several needles with pain killer medicine were attached in both her arms with different monitors buzzing behind her. B and Shad were sitting on Rowi's right side holding her hand and crying.

It took me a while to comprehend everything. I just stood near the entrance of the room staring at Rowi and then at B and Shad. I looked at them, asking the most stupid question. "Why are you both crying? When did they finish with the surgery?" Neither one of them answered my question or even looked at

185

me. I angrily asked the same question again. That's when Shad looked at me and shook his head "no." I didn't understand what the no meant so I asked him again. Shad walked over to me and gently took me in his arms and whispered, "ROWI HAS BEEN SHOT IN THE HEAD. SHE WILL NOT MAKE IT."

I gave Shad an agonizing look, wondering if I heard him right.

"What shit are you talking?" Then I started to raise my voice. "Where is the damn doctor? Why aren't they doing anything?"

Shad made me sit down next to Rowi and then put his hand on mine. "Mom, I spoke to the neurologist. Rowi was shot in the head, there was nothing left to operate on."

I gave Shad a blank look. His words were not being accepted by my brain. "This can't be true, where are the damn doctors and nurses." I shook B by his shoulder, asking him to stop crying and get the medical team. I had definitely lost my mind, not understanding what was happening. It had to be a nightmare or hallucination because this could not be possible in our lives.

I kept pushing Rowi's leg, asking her to get up and stop with the nonsense drama of hers. Nonetheless, in spite of my shouting and screaming, Rowi was still sleeping like an angel.

As people began to hear the horrific news, the hallway outside the ICU was getting packed. Each one praying or trying to offer us solace. Friends offered juice, coffee, water, tissue boxes, or a kind hand or shoulder to cry on. Nobody knew what to do and as the phones rang constantly, I could not pick up or talk to anyone. I was not willing to say that my Rowi might be gone.

I kept saying to myself that she was going to be okay. I would put my head near her legs and then again nudge her legs for her to wake up.

B and I were zoned out, not able to function or answer any questions, Shad had to take the front seat, buckle up, and manage the situation around us.

I just remember closing my eyes and laying my head, with my hands, on her legs. All I kept thinking was, "I have been through so much shit; this cannot be true. Please, oh God, have mercy upon us."

* * *

After midnight, Detective Robert Chisholm came to inform us that Dane Owens had been arrested for attempted murder and aggravated burglary and was booked in Sedgwick County Jail. He added that Dane had said it was an accident. The gun accidentally went off when he was only trying to get her to listen to what he had to say.

I let Detective Chisholm finish, but I was so vexed and distressed I couldn't stop shaking. "Bloody asshole liar" burst from my mouth. "Today he should have been in Manhattan, Kansas, but instead he stayed in Wichita and planned to take her life. THIS WAS NO F'ING ACCIDENT. BLOODY COWARD. Taking her life just because she didn't want to be with him."

I was still shaking when I pulled out my cell and showed Chisholm the text I had sent to Rowi a few days ago. Detective Chisholm read the text message I had sent Rowi warning her to be very careful. The message clearly stated, "I have a feeling Dane Owens is going to hurt you."

Chisholm saw me shaking. He took my hand in his and said, "Don't blame this on yourself. If anyone is to be blamed it's Owens and nobody else. You wouldn't have been able to protect her all the time. If this was his plan, he would have found many other ways to hurt her."

That answer was perhaps logically true but I was grieving so intensely and it offered me no solace or comfort. I was hating myself for not going to the police and seeking some kind of protection. I wish I would have stayed home just to make sure the devil was away from her.

But instead of the warnings from the spirit world, I ignored them and didn't do anything to protect my child. Oh, how I just wanted to die that day.

The next morning, we were bombarded with more calls and visitors at the hospital. I was sitting next to Rowi when I noticed a lady in her mid-sixties with blondish hair standing at the door. I went toward her, and she introduced herself as Debbie Kennedy, CEO of the Wichita's Children Home. Debbie went toward Rowi, touching her forehead and cheeks. I could tell she was saying a quiet prayer for her. She stood there for quite a while caressing Rowi's hand and hair, silent tears pouring out of her eyes.

Debbie then looked at me and said, "Rowena was a gift from God to us. She shared that in her entire life, she had never experienced such a pure soul. More tears were flowing from her eyes, which turned into sobs. I joined in and felt such a sense of pride for how amazing Rowi was. No one had ever said what Debbie had said before. She told us how the girls at the Wichita Children's Home call her Miss Ro or the Selfie Queen. They all love her immensely and she was their Mother Hen.

Debbie continued with her story with a little chuckle. My office is on the first floor. Since Ro was part time, she had never had the opportunity to meet her.

Debbie continued, one day there was a knock at the door but before I could say come in, Ro was standing right in front of her desk, flicking her long hair from her face. I had no idea who this young girl was and asked how I could help her.

Ro was astonished and said, "My name is Rowena, and I am faculty. You don't know me."

Debbie said, before I could ask her anything else she said, "I'm sorry but I don't like your rules."

Debbie again chuckled and said she was amazed with her confidence but peeved with her sassiness. "What is it that you don't like about my rules?"

Ro said, "When my girls work so hard and get good grades the only incentive they have is to watch TV. What kind of stupid incentive is that?"

Debbie said, "What do you suggest?"

Ro said, "Why can't these girls go to a basketball game, have their nails painted, go shopping, or just even some pizza and ice cream?"

Debbie said, "How do you plan to take these girls?" Ro said, "I can drive the eight-seater white van." Debbie had doubts she could reach the pedals, but Rowi already had a solution—she could use cushions if she needed to. Her confidence was strong, and Debbie thought she'd forget the idea, but she did not. There was no stopping Ro. She even used her own salary to help these girls, and it was amazing.

Hearing this was incredible, a bright spot in the darkest day I'd ever had.

Hearing Debbie talk I thought my heart would stop. I reflected on the times when I yelled at Rowi for spending this money, having no idea what she was spending it on.

Rowi would take out money from the ATM and use cash so we wouldn't know where it was spent.

I was filled with guilt and shame at my poor assumptions and negative thoughts. Why didn't I think positive…that she might be doing something good, quietly, which is what I had taught her and Shad since they were children.

Since they had seen so much of distress in our Karachi house for money, I had always taught them to be humble, kind, and respectful. Do things for other people not because of who they are but because of who you are. Be quiet and don't brag about it.

Normally when I spoke to them about such matters the words were greeted with an eye roll. I wish I'd suspected that they had soaked up my advice.

My heart was bleeding for my child, feeling sick to my stomach, always under the assumption who knows Rowi better than I? But sadly, I didn't recognize or understand the other kind and beautiful side of her. I always saw her as Daddy's spoiled little sassy girl.

* * *

For the next few hours Shad had a lot to take on. He had to share the news with his aunts and uncles but the most difficult one was my dad. How could he call his 86-year-old grandpa and tell him his one and only grand daughter's life has been taken?

Instead of calling Dad, he thought it was best to inform Roshan aunty first and ask her how to handle this situation. Roshan aunty suggested that since it was early morning in Karachi, he should call in a few hours, which would give them some time to go to Dad's house, give him some tea and breakfast, and then break the news.

Dad was surprised to see Roshan aunty and Chum uncle at his house by 7:00 a.m. that morning. He knew something was wrong, but he couldn't figure out what it was. He gently looked at Chum uncle and asked what was going on, but the phone rang and Roshan aunty said it was Shad.

Dad quietly heard Shad but was in denial like everyone else. My old father was still grieving for his beloved wife and now his 22-year-old granddaughter.

* * *

Tuesday morning the neurologist was going to perform the Caloric Stimulation test by the late afternoon. Caloric Stimulation is a test that uses differences in temperature to diagnose damage to the acoustic nerve. This test also checks for damage to the brain stem.

When the neurologist came with his team, he explained that when cold water enters the ear and the inner ear changes temperature it should cause fast side to side eye movements called nystagmus. The eyes should move away from the cold water and slowly back. He went on that if there is any slightest brain function left there will be some kind of movement.

The small ICU room was packed with medical staff and Rowi's loved ones praying for her, pleading for mercy on this innocent sweet girl.

B, Shad, and I were right there next to her legs whilst the doctor and his team were starting with the procedure. I could hear my own heart beating so fast, not knowing what to expect. I kept starring at Rowi, anxiously waiting for at least one blink or a slight movement, but my sweet girl Rowi didn't make the slightest move, not even a flick or a blink. The look on the neurologist's face confirmed my thoughts. Her heart was only pumping with the help of the machines.

The doctor pronounced her time of death for 3:40 p.m. on October 4, 2016. That very same day and time a huge part of me died with Rowi.

My 22-year-old best friend, my precious daughter, my sassy full of life baby girl Lola was taken away from me. For the first time in my forty-six years of life, I said, "God, I hate you."

I felt like God had betrayed me. My blind faith and trust were shattered. The only thing that I had always asked for was to keep my children safe and happy, but he didn't keep his word. I vowed to have nothing to do with God anymore.

CHAPTER 34

News of Rowi's death spread like wildfire. Our phones didn't stop ringing and text messages kept buzzing. News Channel KAKE and KWCH of Wichita were doing live coverage outside our house. Our hallways outside the ICU unit were packed with people but it was mostly silent. An older lady came in the unit and asked if she could read a few verses from the Bible. It offered some comfort, even to me and my anger. B's friend asked if he could pray next to Rowi's bed, and we agreed to that as well. No one was denied of anything they wished to do for Rowi and us in their own way.

I remained a bystander though, unable to talk with anyone. All I could do was sit in the chair with my head on Rowi, unrelenting sobs coming out that would not stop. My mind screamed, DANE OWENS, EACH DAY YOU LIVE WILL BE HELL FOR YOU. MAY YOU LIVE FOREVER. This is the curse of a grieving mother.

Detective Chisholm personally came to give his condolences and to inform us that the charges have changed to First Degree murder and aggravated burglary. I remember asking Chisholm what difference it made because it could not change what mattered most—my daughter was not coming back. B's one hand was on my back trying to console me. So much had happened within twenty-four hours, it was just too much to handle.

Chisholm held my hand and said that what I said was true but asked me for strength to fight the case, so he gets the maximum punishment. Don't let him get away so easily. Still holding my hand, he added, "Dane Owens is not your problem, we will handle that for you." Then he looked at B and said, "Just take care of yourselves and your son. Don't forget him in your pain."

That was so true. I had barely spoken to Shad or asked him how he was doing. I was stuck in my own grief that I didn't even think of doing that. Shad and Dua had taken over full responsibility contacting family, talking to doctors, police officers, and making funeral arrangements. Except for Detective Chisholm and a few nurses, I had not spoken to anyone.

* * *

Mehta's arrived late Tuesday evening. They were the first ones to arrive while most of the others were arriving Wednesday evening. Frea and Zarin were absolutely devastated whilst Jumby tried to stay strong for everyone. I held on to Zar for quite a while, crying and sobbing as I relived the horrid accounts from Monday. Frea became very emotional and held on to Rowi for the longest time. I wanted to give some time to Frea and Zar with Rowi. I stepped outside the unit and sat down on the floor, mentally and physically exhausted.

From the corner of my eye, I saw a familiar face walking toward me. As he came closer I realized it was Dr. Mohammed Sandid, one of our parents from Wichita Montessori School. He had just heard the news and personally wanted to meet with us. I held on to Dr Sandid's hand and asked why the doctors had given up so easily on Rowi? Why did they not operate on her? Sandid remained quiet for a while, placed his hand on my shoulder, and said very gently, "Mrs. Irani, the way Rowena was shot, there was nothing left to operate. Even if they would have operated and she would have survived she would have remained like a vegetable for the rest of her life. You do not want to see her like this."

As much as I didn't want to hear the truth at least I was hearing an honest answer. I would have never wanted Rowi to live like a vegetable. She was like my sweet butterfly fluttering from one flower to another. To keep her in a jar would have been painful for her and us. I had to let my sweet angel go to heaven and be peaceful.

* * *

Rowi was an organ donor so they kept her plugged into the machines to keep her organs alive. I clearly remember when she gave her driving test at age 18 and asked to be an organ donor, I had joked with her that you will be 99 by the time you die. Who will need your old organs. I started teasing her how she would look at age 99. Who knew at that time she only had four more years.

By late Tuesday night, B and I reluctantly agreed to go home. Zarin and Frea volunteered to stay with Rowi. Although B and I didn't want to leave her, we were exhausted and needed showers and sleep. From Wesley Hospital to our house B and I were silent, swept up in our own grief and thoughts. My heart was beating so fast, unsure of what would happen or how I would react when I had to look at the crime scene again.

We sat in the garage for a while holding hands, crying, and trying to pick up courage. We could hear Max and Sasha barking near the kitchen door. All we knew was what Shad had told us: Lieutenant Chad Carson, Sergeant Cory Skov, and Officer Chris West from Derby PD had volunteered to feed my babies and take care of the house. Thank you for your kindness!.

When we entered through the kitchen, the first thing I noticed was the carpet with the blood stains had been cut off and a rug from the living room was placed on top.

There was black fingerprint powder everywhere, especially on the front and back doors. They'd been wiped off but the traces still existed.

I noticed that one blind was closed and I opened it up to see why. A bullet had passed through the window and had smashed the glass and the screen. There was also a shell casing on the floor. I wondered why they hadn't taken that away.

* * *

Thoughts of Rowi laying unresponsive on the floor kept me awake. I tossed and turned in my bed before finally going to her bedroom to lay on her bed, snuggling her pillow and blanket. I kept caressing her small teddy bear, which she had since she was a baby. I tucked it in right next to my chest for comfort, but no comfort was to be found.

I finally gave up and went to the living room and laid on the floor where my princess had laid for several hours. Max followed and laid right next to me, Sasha sniffed the area, licked my face and hair, then sat under the dining table. I must have dozed off for a little while but woke up with a pounding headache and immense anxiety.

Moving from the floor to the couch, I sat there and renewed my cries. I still couldn't fathom what was happening. It still seemed like a nightmare, not real.

* * *

It was Wednesday, October 5, when Naz, Cy, Fara and Mehernosh arrived in the evening. A few hours later Naz, came up to me with a startled face. At first, she hesitated but then she said that she was uncertain of how I felt about it but there was a message for me from Diana Farogh. This woman was an empath who was living in Toronto and she had been contacted by Rowi to give us a message. The message was: Please ask my parents to eat.

At that time there was so much going on and too many family members I didn't give it any thought.

Before Rowi's passing, I knew very little about empaths and the spiritual world, never feeling like I had a need to know.

After a month of Rowi's passing Diana did channel Rowi's messages to B. I listened to them but was a bit apprehensive to ask anything.

Forward a bit. One day I was nearly having a nervous break-down because I couldn't stop blaming myself for what had happened and why I didn't do anything to protect her. It was quite late in the evening when Diana messaged B, that Rowi wouldn't let her stay in peace and kept saying mom needs your help, to which I'm not surprised, as when Rowi wants something it has to be done immediately.

Diana asked if she could pick an oracle card for me from "Talking to Heaven" by James Van Praagh. After a lot of shuffling the card that flew out of her hand was: *It's not your fault.*

I was completely blown away and dumbstruck. I never questioned or doubted any messages after that. My door to the spiritual world had opened. The things I had resisted to believe became more clear. I truly believe that Rowi was still very much with us, infact more then she had ever been. She is just in a different dimension. If a message comes in my mind I absolutely believe it's her. Infact the title of the book was also a message from her whilst I was meditating.

To this day, when B, Shad, and I are in our blues we are either surprised by a white pretty feather, butterfly, dragonfly, or cardinal. The most common thing we find is coins in our cars. None of us have ever cashed these coins because of the comfort they offer us; peace and loving reminders of Rowi's ever-lasting presence. Though Rowi is not physically with us she is watching over us and guiding us from her heavenly abode.

There are several special gifts we have received from Rowi but these two still astonishes me.

One day when I found a quarter in the parking lot of my school, I looked at her picture in my car and said, "Rowi for a change can't you send me a dollar bill. About a month later, I was in the basement opening a new pack of toilet rolls. Whilst I was taking out the last one I saw there was something rolled inside the cardboard hole. When I pulled it out, it was a dollar bill. I just couldn't believe it. I threw all the rolls on the floor and ran upstairs screaming, Oh my! "Rowi send me a dollar bill." Behind the bill was written. "May you be blessed with health, wealth and love."

Rowi's bedroom faced East, after I finishing my meditation, I usually stood near the window admiring the sunrise. That particular day the sun was rising just in the middle of a tree.

I went outside and took a picture and sent it to Shad with a Good Morning. After a few minutes, Shad sent a message to enlarge the picture. When I enlarged the picture, there was an arrow. I just couldn't believe what I was seeing. Rowi had an tattoo of an arrow on her left arm.

Though I miss my precious girl, her physical presence and her beauty but I find a bit of a comfort to know she hasn't left, she is very much present and still with us.

CHAPTER 35

Thursday morning the doctors informed us that they were going to take Rowi's organs to prepare for donation. It would be our last day to be with her. I thought to myself there would be planes flying across the US with my baby's organs to save another life. I kept asking, "Why did Rowi have to die so someone else could live?"

Then the time came to wheel her away in surgery room, something shook inside of me like an earthquake. My face was white as a ghost and my hands and knees were shaking as if someone had electrocuted me. The last chance to deny the reality of the moment was gone. Rowi was gone. I felt nauseous and sick to my stomach. I kept holding on to her hand, not wanting to leave her. The nurses started to wheel her toward the surgery room. Fara and Mehernosh were holding on to me, as I could barely walk.

When we reached the door of the surgery room, I held on to her bed and wouldn't let it go. I sat down on the floor holding on to the legs of the bed. B and Shad had to open my grip to let her go. I sat right in front of the door crying and banging for them to open and let me in. I was like a child throwing a tantrum. The doors to the surgery room never opened but instead heaven with angels opened the door for her.

Then came the worst moment for me, the funeral. October 8th was the last time I would be able to see and touch Rowi. Just getting ready for that dreadful moment took a lot of energy. I didn't want to eat and didn't offer any food to my guests either, despite our house being packed. I was drowning in my own sorrows and oblivious to others' needs.

The funeral home looked serene and peaceful. There were beautiful flowers and wreaths from friends, family, and people we didn't even know. There were candles burning behind the coffin. Inside her coffin we had placed her tattered and torn bunny rabbit, which she had since she was a year old.

B and I stood next to her, watching her sleep like a princess from a fairy tale book. She looked radiant with her hair open with a pretty scarf to hide her wounds. I kept standing watching her lay in peace and asking for her forgiveness. I as a mother had failed to save my child from a monster.

The funeral home was packed and the coordinators of Downing and Lahey had to open the side doors, which led to the hallway. Funeral services started right at 10:00 a.m. Jumby gave a brief description on our Zoroastrian religion and the significance of the flame burning in oil.

The two priests, Sirous Felfeli and Sirous Hormazdi, came from Kansas City to perform the funeral prayers. After the prayers, Shad and Debbie Kennedy read their eulogies. Both were deep, beautiful, and wonderfully spoken. Since many of our family members and friends all over the world couldn't come to the US and attend her funeral, with Shad and Debbie's permission I have added their eulogies.

From Shad to his sissy Rowi:

Thank you all for being here today and for your support as we try to make it through these rough days.

When I sat down to write few words for my beloved Rowena. I didn't know what to include. Family members were sitting across the room talking about the happy memories and amazing times we all got to spend and experience with her. The times she made us all laugh so hard we cried, the way she sneezed, and we asked her if she was coughing or sneezing, the way she and I would crack jokes and my mom would sit across the table with a confused look, shaking her head, asking us to explain them.

Rowena was exceptional, unique. When she walked into a room everyone smiled. She was full of life, amazement, and adventure. She was an explorer who wanted to touch the hearts of people wherever she went. She was fearless. Who stood her ground for what she believed in, and fought fiercely for her family and friends in times of need. She never had to be asked to do anything for anyone, she just did it. She was a go-getter. Rowena was enthusiastic, passionate, and radiated positive energy to everyone around her. She was my motivation when I joined the Police Force, she was my strength and courage. She was the pillar of our family who held us all together.

Rowena and I have always had a special bond since the day she came home. We protected each other and had full trust. We'd fight with one another all the time just like any other pair of siblings, we would argue and bicker for hours and when mom would try to interfere, we would team up and tell her to stay out of it, and that it was sibling love. If it got to the point where we needed to go to our own rooms, it would last for about 10 minutes before I would go into her bedroom and ask if she wanted ice cream.

When we were kids, we sat on the floor and played around until Dad got home from work. Dad had this loud off-road motorcycle whose sound was recognized by everyone. Dad would come home, park the bike, walk up the stairs and in the door and find us playing except I would be sitting on the floor looking confused. Rowena would be crying and pointing at me. Guess who got yelled at despite mom and I saying I hadn't done anything. So one day, mom told Dad to switch his bike off and walk it down the street to the house and quietly walk in the door, just to see what would happen. Next day Dad switched his bike off, walked quietly upstairs. Rowena saw him, pointed at me and started crying.

For many years to come Rowena and I grew up together to be one of the closest pair of siblings anyone could imagine. Our morning talks when I dropped her off at JROTC practice, afternoon shenanigans at home driving mom and dad nuts, and our late-night drives to QuikTrip for mango tea. That was our thing.

I remember on my wedding day; she danced and laughed all night. It was the first time I saw her in a saree, and it took by breath away by just how beautiful she looked and how she held on to her saree. I remember the look on her face, just full of happiness and love as my wife and I danced.

As I mentioned before, Rowena was a determined go-getter. When she set her mind to do something she did it. No ifs or buts. There was no one that could convince her to do anything otherwise not even me or Dad. When she started working at the Wichita Children's Home, she was the go-to person ever since she got there. She fought for those girls, made sure that they not only did their homework but did her with them, in a way to lead those girls to success by setting a positive example. I spoke to someone earlier yesterday who said that one of the girls had promised her to finish high school and to further ahead and make a name for herself.

Rowena impacted the lives of countless people in Wichita and several friends and family members all over the world. She still continues to impact the lives of many others, a few of whom she donated her organs to. She still continues to help and keep others alive. It's the only thing she knew, the only way she could be peaceful at the end of the night.

So, I leave you today from this point forward, let Rowena live through you by everything positive you do, every person you help and everyone you are good to. Be happy, enthusiastic, and passionate about life. Appreciate everything you have. Fulfill your dreams. Don't back down because she wouldn't have. Don't let yourself sink because she doesn't want you to. Fight for what you believe in. Let her be the happy memory you think of when something has you down. I promise you it will make you feel better. If you catch yourself doing something out of character and feel like someone tripped you, it was definitely her. But if you are able to catch yourself before you hit the ground, you will know who held you close.

I must say Shad held himself very well, though he did choke up a few times. After his eulogy there was such intense silence and sorrow, only broken by the sobs and sniffles of people there.

After Shad, Debbie Kennedy read her eulogy.

First, I need to thank Rowena's family.

To her parents, you taught your daughter to love life, share with others, and open her heart. To her brother, you lent her your strength and your courage. She brought these gifts you gave her to the Wichita Children's Home, and we were blessed. Thank you!

At the Wichita Children's Home, Rowena who the children loving called Ro, worked directly with children who have been abused, neglected, abandoned and exploited. Children who know traumas, are hurt and afraid to trust. Children who build strong walls and refuse to take them down. Children who refuse to allow anyone into their hearts- however Ro found a way through.

To our children and staff, Ro was a Best friend, a Big Sister, a Mom and a Grandchild.

In addition, she was the Godmother to Gary the fish and a sister to Jeffrey the roly poly. The children talked her into buying them a fish and while they were outside one night, they found a roly poly that she allowed them to bring inside and helped them fix a home for him. By the way, Jeffrey has had babies.

Ro would put her finger in the faces of our children and ask: Have you fed them? While they were having fun with these unusual pets, she was providing them the lesson of how to nurture and care for something more fragile than themselves.

Ro wanted to give the children she cared for, happy childhood memories. She understood that our girls have had rough starts in their lives and need to learn how to be happy children before they can become happy adults. She loved to take our children out on fun adventures: And they WERE adventures.

While she was driving, she danced and sang to the music and make the children sing out loud too. Now you can imagine a van full of teenagers, a pretty women driving, and the van bouncing to the beat of loud laughter and singing. I am sure that when she stopped at traffic lights that many other people in cars alongside her tried to figure out what was going on. What was going on, was she was teaching our youth to enjoy life and live in the moment.

On one of these adventures Ro and the children were at the mall, and it started to rain. Everyone knew Ro didn't like to get her hair wet. As the children and Ro ran to the van to get out of the rain one of the girls tripped and fell. When Ro realized this she ran back to check on the child getting her hair soaking wet. All of a sudden she forgot about her hair and demonstrated to the children that nothing was more important than them.

During academic hour, she studied right along with them, modeling the importance of academic success. The children told me that she would try and help them with their homework but for math she laughed and said ask Google for answers. She taught them the importance of setting goals and figuring out how to achieve them and to believe that anything was possible.

They told me they loved it when she woke them up in the morning because she would enter their room and call them by name, gently shook them awake. Like a very tender mother would do with a child they adored. While doing this she let them know they were loved and valued.

On the days that Ro worked the children told me they couldn't wait to see Ro after school. They wanted to share their day with her. They shared about their boyfriends, their moments of joy and sadness. She listened attentively, letting them know that they were worthy of someone's attention and kindness.

When Children were admitted to the Children's Home, she greeted them like they were the important guests she was waiting for. She showed them around and made them feel special. They instantly knew they were someplace that cared about them.

As I listened to the children talk about Ro, these are the words they used to describe her:

Amazing, Funny, Sweet, Beautiful, Cool, Upbeat, Easy going, Bright, Open Minded, Always Happy, Always Smiling, Memorable.

As the Children were talking about Ro they made promises to always remember the lessons she taught them. As an example, they stated they want to be just like her, never be afraid, be adventurous and courageous. They vowed to become someone she would be proud of. Also to finish High School and go to College. I vowed to seek out more employees like Ro, to do less would mean I didn't learn the lessons she taught me. Ro can never be replaced but she is forever in our hearts.

Thank you Ro for being so kind and loving to the children. Teaching them valuable lessons for life and thank you for being such a great colleague.

Dua had selected very cute pictures and Rowi's favorite songs. One of them was *If I Die Young* by Band Perry and Bollywood song *My Desi Girl* from the movie Dostana. Seeing her pictures made the crowd giggle and cry at the same time.

It took more than an hour for the crowd to come toward the coffin and pay their last respects.

Next the pallbearers came up. They picked up the coffin and placed her gently in the funeral home car.

B, Shad, and I held on to her coffin. We just couldn't let her go. We didn't want her to go. We hugged each other, our hands still on her coffin. There was absolutely nothing in this world, no words, no songs, prayers, or any explanations that would make our pain less or disappear.

I would like to add the Words of Remembrance we had chosen for her Memorial cards.

TOO SOON

This was a life that had hardly begun
No time to find your place in the sun
No time to do all you could have done
But we loved you enough for a lifetime

No time to enjoy the world and its wealth
No time to take life down off the shelf
No time to sing the songs of yourself
Though you had enough love for a lifetime

Those who live long enough
Endure sadness and tears
But you'll never suffer the sorrowing years
No betrayal, no anger, no hatred, no fears
Just love- Only love -In your lifetime

                                        Mary Yandall

CHAPTER 36

With family and friends gone, the pain remained.
The house that had rattled with Rowi and Shad's noise was dead silent. Max was quiet as a mouse and had barely touched his food. The only noise we had was from Sasha barking or the phone ringing.

Rowi's urn was on the mantle of the fireplace next to an oil flame with half dead flowers still in the vase. I had tried to remain strong in front of others but now I was falling apart. I had sleepless nights tossing and turning, the same image of Rowi on the floor kept popping in my head. I still felt responsible for my living nightmare.

After B would fall asleep I often crept into her room and hugged her clothes as tight and as long as I could with silent tears. There were days when I laid on the floor, the exact same place where she had been left so mercilessly for hours.

The word "WHY" was my painful mantra. I kept asking the same questions repeatedly yet answers never came, there was no resolve to be had. I had never asked for a lot from God, only to keep my family safe, healthy, and happy. He'd failed me.

Days turned to months, and time began to move faster. We were all back to work, which was in a way a blessing.

Shad and Dua had made plans to visit my dad in Karachi. They were leaving in March for two weeks. A week before they were leaving Shad asked if he and Dua could move in with us. Without any hesitation, I said yes. I really didn't know if they were in a financial crisis, or he missed home. Whatever the reason he wanted to come home and we were not going to decline his request.

Shad and Dua moved into our basement and left for Karachi within a few days. After their return from Karachi, I could sense a bit of distance between them. I didn't hear any arguments or fights, but it seemed as if they both were just living their own lives. B and I did our best to keep them comfortable. We never asked for any rent or to buy groceries.

No matter how poorly Dua had behaved in the past with us, I didn't treat her the same way. I knew how it felt to be illtreated and had promised myself that I would never act the way my in-laws had acted improperly with me.

I didn't interfere between them and never asked what the problem was. The only thing that really bothered me was when she didn't go to work with the excuse that she was depressed because of Rowi, but would end up going for lunch, shopping, or having her nails done instead. It exasperated us but for Shad's sake it was best to remain quiet. Plus, I didn't have a lot of fight in me.

* * *

Middle of April 2017, we had the preliminary hearing at the Sedgwick County Courthouse. District Attorney Marc Bennett and Assistant District Attorney Alice Osburn had prepared me for the hearing, This was my very first time in a court room and I didn't know what to expect.

Unfortunately, we had to see Dane in court. It broke my heart to see his parents watching their son come into the court room wearing an orange prison jumpsuit, hands handcuffed at the back, and legs in chains.

It was a tragic moment for both the families. It was not his parent's fault and what they were going through was unjust on them.

After hearing the case, Judge Kevin O Conner announced the trial date for September of 2017. Between now and the date of the trial, we found ourselves at court several times. Many plea deals were offered to us, but we refused all of them. No sentence or years seemed enough for the agony and grief he had given not only to us but to so many others who had loved Rowi.

By April 2017, I could see Shad's marriage was falling apart. I perceived that Shad was in too much pain and grief to give Dua the same attention that he used to. Dua wanted her life to be the same as it was before Rowi's death but how could it be the same for Shad or anyone of us.

By May of 2017, it was evident that Shad was in a deep depression. Though he was seeing a therapist his grief for Rowi grew worse. We suggested he get a change of scenery. He agreed and went to Phoenix to see the Mehta family and then went to Hawaii for his cousin's graduation. He went by himself and Dua went out of the country on her own to visit family.

I was relieved when Shad and Dua left. I had tried to be strong for them—a concrete pillar—but I needed a reprieve. Nothing helped me to cope better and I closed up, unwilling to share that grief with others or get help. I felt it was impossible to help me.

Not even sure how I always ended up there, I found myself in Rowi's room once again, reliving memories.

I used to irritate her on weekends when she wouldn't want to get out of bed. I used to lick her cheeks to eventually get her off the bed. She said to me once "Why can't you be like other mothers and nicely wake me up?" So the next day I said, "Wake up my sunshine. My sweet darling baby, it's time to wake up," in a sing song manner.

She pulled down the comforter from her face and said, "Jeez Mom, you don't even know how to fake it." All those lovely precious memories made me smile and then cry too.

* * *

Rowi's favorite destination was Bellows Beach, Hawaii, located in windward Oahu just outside the town of Waimanalo. It is a long thick stretch of white powdered sand facing a clear turquoise blue expanse of ocean.

B and I decided to take Rowi's ashes to Hawaii and lay her rest in the ocean. We flew to Hawaii on June 7th and on Saturday, June 10, we drove to Bellows Beach in the early morning to lay Rowi's ashes. Everyone was quiet and in their own thoughts for the one-hour drive. It was raining cats and dogs from heaven and even the sun was sad and in hiding. I was at the corner seat, my head pressed against the window looking at the grey and black clouds, just wondering how we would lay her ashes in the midst of the storm. Closing my eyes, I started talking to Rowi in my thoughts requesting her to calm the rain. I kept repeating Rowi please help us, Archangel Michael please calm the storms. The storm continued for another thirty minutes, but slowly the heavvy rain turned into light rain and then sprinkles. By the time we got closer to the beach the rain stopped and the sun poked out from behind the clouds. By the time we arrived at 6:30 a.m. the sun was ready to show us its beauty.

Such a heavy downpour but surprisingly the water was calm and warm. B and I held on to her urn for a few minutes, hugging and kissing her last remains. Then all of us took turns to lay her peacefully in the beautiful crystal water.

We held on to her urn, watching as her ashes transferred from the urn to the crystal blue waters and washed out with the tide.

There was a moment of dead silence and teary eyes.

We were all in knee-deep water except for Naz, who was afraid of the water and chose to stand on the beach and hug one of Rowi's pictures.

Out of nowhere, Naz fell on the sand with her legs up in the air. At that moment she reminded me of Humpty Dumpty. It was too funny not to laugh and we all burst out laughing. Perhaps a joke from Rowi to us?

The weirdest part was she kept saying you guys pushed me. Carl said to her, "Are you serious? We were all in the water." Poor Naz, as much as she doesn't like the sand and water, she was covered fully in sand.

We started joking with each other that Rowi didn't want us to cry so she made Naz fall. Whilst we were helping Naz get up and get the sand off her clothes, two cardinals appeared by us. They were hopping around. I had heard that when a cardinal appears an angel is near. I'd never believed it…until that moment.

It was unbelievable to see those cardinals coming so close to us and then following us until we sat in our cars. I truly believe one hundred percent Rowi was there with us to make us laugh and say, "I love you."

Naz and Carl had lived in Hawaii for eight years, but they had never seen a cardinal except on that day: June 10, 2017.

CHAPTER 37

Having Shad and Dua live with us had its pros and cons. I was relieved we got to see him every day, but I missed my personal space. It wasn't their presence as much as it was her siblings being there. They would show up at random times, with disregard for others.

I remember it was a Friday evening, Dua came home with a lot of shopping bags and I was curious but quiet like always. Later when Shad got home and we sat down to dinner, Shad asked Dua how work was.

Dua answered with her head down that she had not gone to work. I wished she would have remained quiet but instead she gave the same answer that she was having nightmares regarding Rowi.

In an instant, Shad was enraged. He banged his hand on the table so hard—all our plates shook. "ENOUGH! You will not blame my sister just because you don't want to go to work. My parents work without missing a day, I work but you can't, but then instead you go shopping."

He pushed his chair out and ran downstairs. Dua was very embarrassed and followed him. B and I didn't say a word and quietly finished our food. At that point in time, we both knew that this marriage was not going to last very long.

Within days, B and I were watching TV and we heard the kitchen door open and close a lot. I wanted to find out what was happening but B stopped me. Shortly later a car pulled out and I had no idea if one or both of them had left.

Shad answered that question for me. He came into our bedroom. "Dua has left to stay at her friend's house for a few days, we both need some time to ourselves. She will be back when we both are ready."

What could we say? Nothing would have helped.

It was June 22, my sister's birthday; that's how I remember the exact date. I was not at home when Dua came to take all her stuff from our house to move into an apartment with her sister.

Next month in July, Dua texted Shad and said she wanted a divorce. I don't know if that was an impulsive decision or intentional, but I do know those are not things you state over a text message. Shad texted her back asking when and where to sign.

After the text, B was trying to convince Shad to get a lawyer for himself. But he was stubborn and convinced that since they didn't have any children, house, or bank accounts together it would be easy, not necessary.

We tried convincing him that no divorce was as peaceful as people thought it should be. Emotions were high. Anger was often too real. Revenge and entitlement existed. But Shad didn't listen.

* * *

August of 2017, B and I flew to Karachi to attend Rowi's first Farvardegan—or Muktad prayers—and to visit my dad.

Zoroastrians all over the world celebrate the last ten days of their religious calendar. We believe that during Muktad days, we have to remember their own departed ones. The fact is that Muktad are days for the collective worship of all Fravashis, followed by the remembrance of individual souls of your dearly departed ones.

After the ten days prayers were over, Dad's deteriorating health took its toll. He had been in the hospital for a month due to old age complications and depression. Dad was in and out of consciousness, his heartbeat was erratic. The doctors didn't know if he'd make it through the night or not. I stayed with him that night, not having the heart to leave him by himself. My aunt SHE arrived from London on August 20th, but by that time Dad was unconscious. I wish she would have come just a few days earlier so at least he could have seen her.

Dad passed away peacefully on August 21st, just twenty-one days after his 87th birthday. SHE, B, and I were there with him when he passed away. Fara and Shad were arriving that same night, thankfully in time for the funeral in the morning.

* * *

August 21st started as a normal bright sunny day, but by late evening we had torrential rain with high winds. I have never seen this kind of weather in Karachi before.

There was no electricity and many tree limbs had fallen on the main roads taking down electric lines with it. With the pothole filled streets it was dangerous as well as treacherous.

B and I got the chance to attend two of his evening prayers at our temple but we left before the fourth day early morning prayers. Typically, in our religion we have prayers at our temple for ten days, then the first month, six months, Muktad prayers, and first anniversary.

After B and I left for Wichita, Fara, Shad, and SHE were still in Karachi for another week. It was good for all three to be together after a long time. Shad was happy he had made the trip five months ago to see his Grandpa. He was a young man of twenty-six who had lost two of the most important people from his life and was in the midst of a divorce.

Shad returned from Karachi with renewed grief at what he'd lost. A week later, he received his divorce papers. There was another document attached—one asking for alimony.

Shad was infuriated and heartbroken that Dua had not kept her word. He angrily picked up the phone, eager to give her hell, but thankfully B was at home and stopped him. If he lashed out it would surely go against him. He was so upset—enraged actually—and near the point of a breakdown. There was no calming him down.

B contacted me at work and asked if there were any parents who were attorneys. I just couldn't think straight but asked my friend Kelly Wilson if she knew someone.

We were able to find a divorce lawyer who was busy but would help Shad.

It may have been Shad's divorce, but it felt as if our lives were on hold. Nothing was moving forward. All three of us were still struck in grief and stress. Each one of us were crying and yelling from the inside while trying to be outwardly strong for others.

Many of our friends and family suggested to move out of the house we were in—maybe even out of state—but I didn't have the energy or motivation to look for another job or house. I wasn't ready to leave Wichita before justice was served to my child.

CHAPTER 38

October 4, 2017, one year without Rowi. For twelve months, I hadn't seen her or heard her voice. But every day I wrote a letter to her, just wrote whatever my heart wanted me to say to her. I felt like as if there were many things unspoken and left behind.

I'm sharing a very personal letter that I wrote to my baby girl. I get a lump in my throat when I read it to this day.

One year ago, the angels took you to heaven. You were so special; they didn't want to leave you behind.

The heartless evil beast took you away from us, not stopping or thinking for a minute, he was taking a precious life.

I have screamed, yelled, cried, and begged but nothing brought you back.

I should have said I LOVE YOU, kissed and hugged you million times more. I'm sorry I wasn't there to protect you. I'm sorry you had to be alone for so long. I'm sorry I wasn't the best mom. I should have stayed home on October 3rd to protect you. Oh, dear God, why did I not do that. Why did I not take any protection from police?

Now you are in Heaven where no one will ever hurt you. I'm sure it's beautiful and peaceful. I love it when you send me feathers, coins, and butterflies. I know it's a gift from you.

Please ask God to call me soon to you. I'm tired, torn, and broken, and cannot do this anymore.

I LOVE YOU TO THE MOON AND BACK A MILLION TIMES MY BABY GIRL, MY LOLA.

For her first death anniversary, we had requested Sirous Felfeli come in from Kansas City for the prayers. Zar came from Phoenix too. On the same day we had a navjote ceremony for Shad to bring him back in our Zoroastrian religion.

The Navjote ceremony is a ritual through which only Zoroastrian children have a ceremony in which they begin to wear a sudreh (a religious white cotton undergarment) and kushti (thread made of sheep wool). Shad, Rowi, and Frea had their navjote in 2001 but since Shad had changed his religion, he had to have his navjote done again. Zar stayed with us for a few days, then she headed back to Phoenix. It was nice to have new energy in the house and to hear another set of stories about sweet Rowi.

* * *

Shad's divorce was finalized in November of 2017.

I was at work but B went with Shad to the court hearing. The judge asked Shad to pay $1,000 in installments for 3 months or pay the whole amount upfront. B didn't want to get into the installment confusion and paid the whole amount upfront. Until this day I don't fully understand why Shad had to pay her any money but there is no arguing a judge's decision. Dua was out of our lives and that was good. Until she wasn't…

Dua accused Shad of stalking her at work and her home. He was so angered and flabbergasted because this impacted his work. There was even a restraining order filed against him.

All these accusations were false, of course, and it took a long time for that to be proven. However, those blatant lies were easily disproven, but not without more stress on Shad and all of us, really.

As the investigation happened, Shad didn't hesitate to ask the detective to investigate everything. He had nothing to hide and the last person he ever hoped to see was Dua. There was an exhaustive and comprehensive internal affairs investigation held by both departments checking his cell phone, body, and on-board vehicle cameras, and GPS history, along with miles counted for those particular days Dua claimed he'd stalked her.

Based on the results of the investigation, the City of Derby paid for Shad's defense attorney to fight the allegations in court. The only reason why the Chief of Derby paid for the attorney because he had not only known Shad as a police officer but also as a student at Wichita State, where he had taught criminal justice in those days.

The first court hearing was on September 14th, but Shad's lawyer needed some more time because Dua refused to provide any paperwork that was requested.

Shad's lawyer applied to have the case dismissed, but Dua hired a lawyer at the last minute to keep the case moving. However, with no evidence or basis to her claims, the case was dismissed with a civil order stating that Shad could not have any contact with anyone from his ex's family, unless it was done so in an official capacity while Shad was on duty.

After all the senseless fights and arguments, Shad realized his mom had been correct. It meant nothing and more than anything I was sure glad it was over. There was a bigger and more pressing trial awaiting us all.

With Shad's debacle done, it was time to return to the courthouse for the trial of Rowi's murderer. It had been a long wait.

* * *

The date was October 31, 2018. At the trial there were twenty-three witnesses. Our Judge was Kevin O' Conner, with District Attorney Marc Bennett and Alice Osburn.

Leading up to that morning I prayed endlessly to God to give strength to all family members and our friends who were going to be present in the court. It was going to be heart wrenching to see Dane again, and to relive everything that I had hidden inside of me to feign normalcy and healing. There really is no way to do that, I later discovered.

I was nervous but yet ready to send the man to prison forever. The jury selection took a while and that was okay. You do need the right people for these situations.

Finally, at 2 p.m. the trial started. I was very surprised to see the size of the courtroom. At the entrance of the courtroom, on the right-hand side there were three long uncomfortable wooden benches. Security wouldn't let anyone sit on the first row as it was too close to Dane and his defense attorney. Right next to the defense attorney's table were our prosecutors. Left of the entrance door a little further up were chairs for twelve jurors from which seven were males and five females, ranging from the ages of twenty-five to sixty-five.

Dane was brought in the courtroom handcuffed but in civilian clothes. His handcuffs were taken off as he was seated. After everyone settled down, Judge Kevin O'Conner entered the noiseless courtroom.

The judge talked a bit, swore in the jury, and explained their responsibility. Then Mrs. Osburn started with her opening statement.

She talked about Rowi and everything she was preparing to do in life, as well as why she had broken up with Dane, who wanted more from Rowi than she was prepared to offer.

I listened to every detail of my precious Rowi's life that was spoken, sometimes fearing to look at the defendant and other times just seething at him. I don't know how I expected him to act. Nothing would have made me feel better.

Then I relived one of the most tragic moments of my life over again. Mrs. Osburn talked about how Dane abandoned calling authorities after he shot her. Why did he do that if it was an accident? He chose to leave Rowena laying there severely wounded for several hours, until I found her and called for help.

After Mrs. Osburn finished with her opening statement, the defense attorney started with the fact that Dane Owens is adopted. His parents adopted him when he was a few months old. After high school, Dane wanted to serve his country and joined the US Army. He was deployed twice to fight the ongoing war in Afghanistan. He was a fine and brave soldier, doing everything possible to keep his fellow soldiers safe.

Oh, yeah, I thought, Dane is also a stone-cold killer.

The defense attorney continued on and stated his case, then asked for a minimum sentence.

Minimum! I couldn't believe it.

After that, I was the first witness. I had been through so much shit, but I had never imagined that one day I will be sitting in a US court room fighting for justice.

After I was sworn in Mr. Bennett began to ask his questions:

Mr. Bennett: *Can you please tell me your name?*
Toranj: *My name is Toranj Irani.*

Bennett: *Where are you employed?*
Toranj: *Wichita Montessori School.*

Bennett: *How many years have you worked there?*
Toranj: *This is my thirteenth year.*

Bennett: *Where do you live?*
Toranj: *2612 Meadow Oaks Ct.*

Bennett: *Which two streets would you use to your neighborhood?*
Toranj: *29th and Woodlawn. We can also take 29th and Oliver Street.*

Bennett: *How many children do you have?*
Toranj: *Two children. Rooshad is my son and Rowena is my daughter.*

Bennett: *How old was Rowena?*
Toranj: *Rowena was twenty-two years old.*

Bennett: *What does your son do for a living?*
Toranj: *Rooshad is a police officer at Derby PD.*

Bennett: *At that time did Rooshad live with you?*
Toranj: *Rooshad was married and lived with his now ex-wife.*

Bennett: *What does your husband do?*
Toranj: *My husband Behram works for Dillons Marketplace at Central and Rock Road.*

Bennett: Was Rowena a student?

Toranj: Yes, she was a junior at Wichita State University studying Psychology.

Bennett: Apart from studying was she working?

Toranj: Yes, Rowena was working at the Children's Home and was also a student Ambassador.

Bennett: Did everyone in the house have a fixed schedule?

Toranj: Since everyone was working and Rowena at university everyone had a fixed schedule.

Bennett: How many cars do you have?

Toranj: We have two cars.

Bennett: So you have three adults but two cars?

Toranj: Rowena has her own car to go to WSU and work, but my husband and I share the car. Since he works at Dillons, which is a mile from my school, he drops me off and then goes to work. I also work After School Program but every other week. The week I have ASP, Behram finishes his work and picks me up at 6pm. The days I am off from ASP then Rowena picks me up at 3:15 pm. Thankfully week of October 3rd, 2016, it wasn't my week.

Bennett: What happened on October 3rd, 2016?

Toranj: October 3rd, 2016, started as a normal day. I made her usual breakfast which is cold coffee and bagel with cream cheese. At 7:15 am I went to her bedroom in the basement, woke her up, told her your breakfast is ready, kissed her forehead and said bye. My husband and I left for work at 7:20 am.

Bennett: *What happened at 3:30 pm when she didn't come to*
           pick you up?
Toranj: *Behram called me around 3:15 pm asking if Rowena*
           had come to pick me up. I said no not yet but she will.
           His voice sounded worried. Behram said I have been
           trying to call her since 1pm, but her cell keeps going
           on voicemail. When he said that I started panicking
           and called her too.

Mr. Bennett placed a beautiful picture of Rowena on the table. Same picture could be seen by jury on the big flat TV screen mounted on the wall.

Rooshad had chosen this particular picture because it was full length in which you could estimate her height and body weight. This picture was taken on her first day back at WSU as a sophomore. In this picture her long brown hair is open, and she is wearing a cotton kurta. I remember asking her to smile and as usual my sassy girl had given me a very cheeky smile.

Bennett: *Do you recognize her?*

At this point I went down the road of memory lane and broke down. I couldn't hold on to my emotions any longer. I kept touching her picture and sobbed.

Mr. Bennett came and stood right next to me, poured a glass of water, and asked if I needed time. I begged God and Rowi to give me strength. After a few minutes, I recollected myself and asked them to go on.

Bennett: *Since Rowena didn't come to pick you up what did*
           you do?
Toranj: *I took a ride home with my co-worker Jennifer Flem-*
           ming.

Bennett: *Was anyone else in the car besides Mrs. Flemming and you?*

Toranj: *Yes, her 10 year old daughter at that time was also in the car.*

Bennett: *Did Mrs. Flemming park on the street or driveway?*

Toranj: *Jennifer parked on the driveway.*

Bennett: *How did you enter the house since you didn't have the garage opener?*

Toranj: *I punched in the garage code which is on the left-hand side of the door.*

Bennett: *Once the garage door was open what did you see?*

Toranj: *I saw Rowena's car parked at her normal spot.*

Bennett: *Which part of the house do you enter from the garage door?*

Toranj: *We enter into the kitchen.*

Bennett: *What did you see when you entered the kitchen?*

Toranj: *When I entered the kitchen, I saw Rowena lying in a pool of blood. Sasha and Max sitting next to her.*

Bennett: *Which area of the house was she in?*

Toranj: *Rowena was lying near the dining room table. Her head was facing the south and her legs toward the north.*

Mr. Bennett took out a diagram of the house that was done professionally and asked me to explain the layout starting from the garage door.

Toranj: Entering the kitchen I'm facing East. On my left is the door to the pantry. On my right is the stove and countertops. In the middle is the kitchen island. Where I'm pointing is the dining table facing the back door, still facing East.

Still pointing to the diagram, I showed where Rowena was laying.

Bennett: *What was she wearing?*

Toranj: *Rowena was wearing her blue jeans and a shirt. Her dark blue scarf was lying next to her.*

Bennett: *When you saw Rowena lying in a pool of blood what did you do?*

Toranj: *When I saw Rowena lying in a pool of blood, I started screaming her name. I said, "Rowena, Rowena, what happened? But there was no response. I ran back to the back door pushed Jennifer from the kitchen door. I didn't want her daughter to see Rowena. I began screaming call 911. Oh God what has happened in this house.*

Bennett: *When Mrs. Flemming was calling 911 what did you do?*

Toranj: *I was in a shock and nervous, didn't know what to do, so I picked up her scarf and pressed it on the wound which was on her head. I called my husband who was on his way home. I started screaming, "Rowi is covered in blood and not responding."*

My husband started yelling call 911. Then I called.

Rooshad, he didn't pick up the first time but responded the second. I was hysterically shouting at him: Rowi is in a pool of blood. I don't know what to do. Oh God why isn't anybody coming.

Bennett: *Mrs. Flemming made the 911 call. Did you also call 911?*

Toranj: *Yes, I did. Seeing Rowena laying there, and no help was coming fast, I panicked and ran to the home phone and made a call to 911 as well.*

Bennett: *What did you do after making that call?*

Toranj: *After making the 911 call my stomach felt very upset. I had no choice but to leave her alone and use the bathroom. Whilst I was in the bathroom, I could hear people in my house. I knew then EMS and police had arrived.*

It was Defense Lawyer's turn to ask. He pointed at the diagram of the house.

DL: *When you enter the house what is on your right-hand side?*

Toranj: *I am pointing at the entrance and showing that on the right-hand side are the stairs to the basement.*

The reason he asked this question was because the police officers had found a shell casing on the ledge of the basement stairs.

There were no more questions for me.

More or less the same questions were asked to Jennifer Flemming.

After questioning her there was a video shown of Dane entering and leaving the neighborhood.

The next witness was Casey Adams. He was a good friend of Rowena's. They had been texting on the day Rowi died. She had sent Casey a picture of Sasha outside. That was at 12:57 pm.

That message was the last one that Casey ever received from Rowena. It was not the last time he saw her, however.

On the evening of October 3, 2016, Casey shared that he was at the ER Westley Medical Center, where he worked. They got a patient with a gunshot wound to the head. The gunshot wound was so deep that a lot of blood had been lost too. They knew the patient wouldn't survive.

Then Casey saw the name tag on her hand. He was shocked and in disbelief. Who would want to hurt an innocent girl like Rowena?

Facing the jury, Mr. Bennett said, "Please note. Rowena's last text to Mr. Adams was at 12:57 p.m. A picture of Sasha the dog. Rowena was shot inside her home. As we see in the video, Dane left the neighborhood at 1:05 p.m. Mr. Dane came inside, shot Rowena, took her phone, and left through the back door. His intention was not to talk but to kill her.

After Casey Adams gave his statement, Officer Brooke Rosenboom from Wichita State University was asked if Rowena attended her classes at WSU on October 3, 2016.

Officer Rosenboom confirmed by professors that she had been in school. Then there was the testimony of Officer Henry, who had been asked to go to Mr. Dane's house by his supervisor.

It is the video of Dane in that officer's car that still haunts me to this day.

When Officer Henry reaches Dane's house he knocked several times, then a groggy, shirtless, and barefooted Dane opened the door.

Officer Henry asked Dane to put his shirt on and told him there was an incident with his ex-girlfriend and that he needed to cooperate and go with him to the Wichita Police Station downtown, where the detectives were waiting for him.

Officer Henry checked the garage and saw a silver-colored Nissan Frontier parked in the garage. The same vehicle that we had seen in the video.

Before taking Dane to the Police Station, Officer Henry had asked Butler County EMS to check his vitals. Everything was normal.

A video was turned on when they got into the car for the twenty-five-minute drive. Officer Henry asked Dane which school he graduated from, how many siblings he had, which sport he played, which was his favorite football team. Dane was happily answering all his questions.

I was running out of patience and getting irritated, that not even once he asked about Rowena. He had taken an innocent girl's life for no reason and there he was joking and talking with the officer as if nothing had happened.

I whispered into B's ear, "SERIOUSLY, why do we have to watch this crap." B whispered back Officer Henry is purposely asking nonstop questions just to prove his brain is functioning 100% and he is capable of answering all the questions that the detective will ask. After hearing this, the two-hour video made sense. I still feel repulsed by the thought of that video to this day.

One defense witness I found to be very interesting was Sergeant Frye, and that's why I have added his entire testimony. Pay particular attention to the ending.

DL: *Could you please tell us your name?*
S.   *Frye: My name is Steve Frye.*

DL: *What do you do for a living?*
S.   *Frye: I'm an infantryman in the Army.*

DL: *Where are you based now?*
S.   *Frye: Fort Bragg, North Carolina.*

DL: Do you know Dane Owens?
S.   Frye: I do know him.

DL: How do you know him?
S.   Frye: He served under me. I was his first line supervisor for roughly two years, on and off.

DL: Were you also—what's squad leader?
S.   Frye: A squad leader is usually a staff sergeant in charge of a nine-man infantry squad, in charge of two sergeants and six other individuals.

DL: Would you have been Dane's squad leader as well?
S.   Frye: Yes sir.

DL: What kind of soldier was Dane Owens?
S.   Frye: So the fine thing about Dane is he came in during what we call the surge. It was 2008, 2009 when the President was sending as many troops as he could to Afghanistan, so that right there showed courage. He was the first group of new privates that we got when I got back from my first deployment. Out of the bunch, he was the most in shape and motivated, he spent about a year with me for train up in the platoon.

DL: What is Barge Matal?
S.   Frye: Barge Matal is a battle, referred to now as the Battle of Barge Matal. It's a low ground. It's split by a fast-moving river and there's a high ground on all four sides. It was a very excluded area, and it was mainly manned by Afghan National Police who weren't that well trained, so it wasn't just regular Taliban that took it over, it was someone else and I think a little bit of Taliban as well. They swept in one night and killed all the A&P folks.

DL: What is A&P?

S. Frye: The Afghan National Police. We were spun up to respond to that.

DL: How old was Dane when all this was going on?

S. Frye: Nineteen at the most.

DL: What was his position at Barge Matal?

S. Frye: At that time, he was a machine gunner.

DL: By pulling security on the far side, what do you mean by that? What was he doing?

S. Frye: So the technique we use is if a vehicle hits an IED, or an improvised explosive device, the first thing you want to do is get a vehicle on both sides of it. That's probably the most important thing to do.

DL: Is that to protect the man in the downed vehicle?

S. Frye: Yes, Sir. The platoon medic can start assessing casualties and moving people around.

DL: When Dane pulled it around to that position how did he perform at that point?

S. Frye: Dane did absolutely everything he needed to do. He started scanning. There are multiple different platforms inside the vehicles that we can use to scan around, and he used them all. He was an expert on all of them. He was giving the gunner commands or truck commander was out moving around. You can't trust everybody to be able to take charge of that. That's a heavy weapon system that can inflict many casualties in a short time, BUT Dane WAS RESPONSIBLE ENOUGH TO BE TRUSTED WITH THAT WEAPON SYSTEM.

CROSS- EXAMINATION

Bennett: Let's talk about training. Being in the Army, how long is basic training?

S.   Frye: When I went it was sixteen weeks but now, they are moving to twenty-two.

Bennett: So, when you first met Dane, he had been through basic?

S.   Frye: Yes, that's correct.

Bennett: During basic training, you train them to do many things but amongst them is to utilize the weaponry of war?

S.   Frye: That's correct.

Bennett: How much training does one have to have? Is it like a 14-week course kind of a thing you go through to be infantry trained?

S.   Frye: No. So as soon as you finish up basic training and advanced individual training at Fort Benning as an infantryman, you will probably get ten days of leave and then come straight to your unit. You will process the division which at the time was the Tenth Mountain Division and you will get sent to your unit, that's where Dane meets me.

Bennett: It's your testimony that Dane, through all that training from basic, to JRTC, through the daily training in your platoon got to the point where on numerous occasions he handled himself well during pressure situations?

S.   Frye: That's correct.

Bennett: Do you have any idea how many times or how many rounds would have shot through his weapon during the time he was serving with you?

S. Frye: It takes about 25.000 rounds to qualify forty men, or forty soldiers on a range in one day. It takes 40 rounds for one soldier to qualify, if they are good. He probably shot about that range 25.000 in training.

Bennett: How are you all trained to treat your weapon?

S. Frye: LIKE THEY ARE LOADED AT ALL TIMES.

Bennett: Are they supposed to aim it at something that you don't intend to kill?

S. Frye: NO, SIR.

Bennett: Are you trained repeatedly about that?

S. Frye: Yes, Sir.

Bennett: When you are moving around each other, you are not always spanned out. I assume in the field there are going to be times that you are traveling, walking in close proximity, just given the terrain you encounter. Are you supposed to move around each other in close proximity with a finger on the trigger? Or how do you manage not to shoot one another when you are in close proximity?

S. Frye: So, a lot of times, the training does come back to you. You do remember, before I get up and start running around to throw my weapon on safe really quick. Sometimes you forget and you get lucky, but for the most part as infantryman trains, you don't really have that problem so much.

Bennett: The job you are trained to do over and over again is to be a trained...someone who is trained to enter into battle and kill when necessary?

S. Frye: Close with and destroy the enemy.

Bennett: To do that task appropriately, this training has to be
second nature?

S. Frye: Absolutely.

Bennett: So you instinctively know when to put your finger
on the trigger and when to keep it away from the
trigger?

S. Frye: On the M4 series rifle, the m249 SAW, and the M240
Bravo. Yes sir.

Bennett: What if someone were to hand you a weapon that
you weren't trained with, you would know to treat
it the same as something you trained on back
then?

S. Frye: If someone handed me a weapon that I didn't normally
use, I would instruct and ask them how to clear it.

Bennett: Sure.

S. Frye: But we don't normally train on pistols.

Bennett: I understand. But the pistol is a weapon.

S. Frye: It is a weapon.

Bennett: With as much respect as the M14 or any other weapon
you've trained with?

S: Frye: Yes Sir.

Bennett: Is Dane a left-handed shooter?

S: Frye: Yes Sir.

Bennett: There are times when one of your men, for that matter
somebody in the Afghan forces, would be injured by
the Taliban. Did you encounter that? People on your
team getting hurt?

S. Frye: Yes Sir.

Bennett: *So, in addition to the training about how to handle weaponry were you trained about how to respond to a person who had been injured near you by a gunshot wound or with some other device?*

S. Frye: *Yes Sir.*

Bennett: *Don't want to Hollywood this, but the old phrase: Never leave a man behind. Does that have some meaning to you as a soldier in the theater of war?*

S. Frye: *It's what we live by.*

Bennett: *So, if somebody is injured, are you trained to attend to them; attend to the person who is injured in front of you?*

S. Frye: *Yes Sir.*

Bennett: *Is there actual training that goes with it? Not just pick a guy up and running to the back. Do you get trained on how to attend the wounds and how to deal with someone that's on your team who may have been injured?*

S. Frye: *Yes Sir. Combat Casualty Care.*

Bennett: *Is that also drummed into you in training?*

S. Frye. *Yes.*

Bennett: *It's got to be a stressful situation to see someone you know, and you have worked beside. You have to maintain your cool to help them and attend to them?*

S. Frye: *Yes.*

Bennett: *So, if there is someone that you see who is injured, but should be at this point instinctual, to size up their injuries and seek help for them and attend to those injuries if you are there and you see this person who is hurt?*

S. Frye: *Yes, Sir.*

Bennett: Mr. Dane would have had that same training to again attend to someone who has been injured?

S. Frye: Dane definitely attended the combat lifesaver course which teaches you how to administer IVs and place tourniquets and drag a casualty to cover.

Bennett: Thank you Sir. I appreciate it.

The trial didn't end with Sergeant Frye. There were many more witnesses after him. Sergeant Frye's good remarks regarding Dane, to be a fine soldier, didn't match with any of his character on October 3, 2016. According to Sergeant Frye he said we never leave our men behind, but yet Dane deliberately left my daughter to die.

The trial concluded on November 8, 2018.

Unfortunately, jurors didn't see it as premeditated murder. Dane was convicted of first-degree felony murder and aggravated burglary.

December 20, 2018 was the day of the sentencing. It was the very last day I had to be in the Sedgwick County Court House and the last time I would ever lay eyes on him.

Dressed in an orange jumpsuit, head shaved, hands and legs handcuffed and chained to his legs, he sat down beside his defense lawyer.

The defense lawyer started the opening statement that he has received many letters from Dane's family and friends, stating what a wonderful man he has always been. Never got in trouble with the law before, served in Afghanistan war and developed PTSD. October 3, 2016, he had taken many pain-killers, much more than the normal dose. The defense lawyer shared all of this, showing he was pleading to the judge for a lesser sentence.

After hearing the defense lawyer, Judge Kevin O'Conner asked Mr. Bennett if the victim's family would like to say something. Mr. Bennett said, "Rowena's mother and brother would like to be heard for the first time after the tragedy."

I walked toward where Mr. Bennett was standing. I had requested not to be on the camera by the media, so instead of the witness box, I was standing next to Mr. Bennett, which actually favored me as some sort of support.

I had to take a few deep breaths and control my emotions. I started talking about the horrific days of October 3rd and 4th, 2016.

My voice was getting loud and angry as if I was demanding answers. I looked directly at the judge and asked what did Rowena do that was so wrong that she lost her life? All she did was say no to their two-month long relationship. They were not dating for years. Why did she have to lose her life? Why did he punish Rowena and us so severely?

"Mr. Dane, it was not okay for you to enter our neighborhood, my house, without asking permission and taking my daughter's life for absolutely no reason. What did you think you will get away with this, just because she was born in Pakistan? Your Defense Attorney made it quite clear to the jury at the trial instead of being respectful and taking her name he kept saying this Pakistani girl, that Pakistani girl, and even said that what are the odds, Mr. Dane fought a war in Afghanistan, which is the neighboring country with Pakistan. Mr. Dane ex-girlfriend was from Pakistan too.

"So what if she was a Pakistani. Are you trying to say it's okay to take a Pakistani girl's life? No, It's not okay to take anyone's precious life.

"You, Mr. Dane, made this choice, nobody made this decision for you. Trust me when I tell you after thirty-four or thirty-five years, I will be dead and gone but when you are eligible for parole, Rooshad will be right there in your face, telling or father begging parole board members why you shouldn't get out of prison. I hope you rot in prison every single day for the rest of your life."

Then the one egregious, disrespectful, and repeated offense of the Defense Attorney was addressed. "One last thing I would like to say to the defense attorney, her name is Rowena, I will spell it out for you. R-O-W-E-N-A NOT ROWANA OR ROWANDA. DON'T EVER FORGET THIS NAME: ROWENA BEHRAM IRANI."

After I finished with my sentencing speech Shad went and stood next to Mr. Bennett. He didn't want to be photographed or videoed either.

"Judge, I don't know what else to say that my mother hasn't already said. I knew this man five years. I trusted him to date my sister. She was my only sibling, my parent's only daughter, and my grandparent's only granddaughter.

"I was the one who had to make the phone call to my grandfather thousands of miles away and tell him Rowena had been shot and was not going to live. My grandfather didn't even make it for a year after that.

"It is beyond my understanding why the jury didn't find him guilty of premeditation. He brought his gun down from Manhattan, left the house on a Monday morning knowing his parents were out of state. He knew no one would be at my house, parked the car down the street, waited for her to come home, walked to the house, let himself in, and shot her. He grabbed her phone and walked out through the back door.

"Not once did he ask the officers if Rowena was okay and if she had lived. It was all about his issues and problems, nothing about Rowena. I work for the system every single day. I fail to understand why he was given the right to spend two years defending what he did, when my sister wasn't given a chance to defend her own life.

"Dane Owens I will be there for every parole board meeting and if you ever get out I will be waiting for you."

In addition to our statements, columnist Amy Renee Leiker from the Wichita Eagle newspaper wrote there was no evidence to support claims that military-induced PTSD was behind a beloved Wichita State student's 2016 slaying. This is her article:

> *This isn't about a soldier suffering from post-traumatic stress syndrome. This is a case of a jilted boyfriend, who could not accept that the person he wanted to be with didn't want to be with him.*
>
> *As a soldier was trained and knew what would happen when you pulled the trigger on a firearm." Judge Kevin O' Conner said, noting that Dane claim the gun discharge accidentally wasn't consistent with physical facts of the case.*
>
> *"This is murder. And this was the taking of another person's life," the judge said. "A young person who had her whole life ahead of her."*
>
> *Owen's life sentence carries parole eligibility after he serves 25 years. If he is granted parole, he will have to serve the additional 43 months before he can be released from prison.*

I don't know what life has in store for Owens but I know my life, my family's lives, will never be the same. The grief, guilt, and pain is permanently embedded. I cannot help but still wonder what the price of a life is worth. Nothing can adequately prepare a parent to answer that question about their child.

CHAPTER 39

Several months after Rowi's passing I received a sweet letter from Emily. She was Rowi's liver recipient. All I knew at that time that she was 37, a mother of two children, and had a boyfriend.

But four years later on what would have been Rowi's 27th birthday, Emily, her then fiancé Jim, her daughter Emma, mom Katherine, sister Kate, Kate's husband Doug and their daughter Maley, drove all the way from Colorado to meet with us and celebrate her birthday.

I had waited four long years to meet Emily. Just the fact that some part of Rowi was still alive living in another person's body. How Rowi's gift had given a new life to Emily, who may not have made it.

Emily is a beautiful woman inside and out, with gorgeous blue eyes and blonde hair. Despite her shyness, it was important for her to learn about Rowi and her life. B, Shad, and I were filled with smiles and tears as we talked nonstop about Rowi and her quirkiness, laughing as we warned Jim that if Emily acts weird it's not her but most certainly is Rowi.

This is Emily's story. A true reality with the gift of life.

In 2002 shortly after my son was born, I began to have severe itching around my body. After many different soaps and laundry detergents the problem wasn't being solved. After have some lab work done, the results showed that my liver enzymes was elevated. After several visits to the specialist, several misdiagnoses and trips to Mayo Clinic, I was told I had Primary Sclerosing Cholangitis, an auto immune disease of the bile ducts in the liver. I was told there was no cure and that a transplant could be a factor at some point in the future. I was 23 at that time and couldn't possibly believe that I, someone that had been healthy would ever get to the point of needing a transplant. I moved forward almost living in denial that I was sick.

In 2010 I had to stop working. I felt completely defeated and several times I told my mom, "I want to die." I didn't want to continue living like this. PSC had stolen my life and the person I wanted to be. Most difficult was my inability to be fully involved in my children's lives, while at the same time being so thankful I had them in my life, which kept me fighting with this disease and not giving up easily.

In 2014 a visit with my doctor determined that having a liver transplant would be the next step. I went through the transplant evaluation, which was approved but I left myself inactive on the list for several months. Needing a transplant seemed surreal to me and I was scared to go through such a big surgery. But PSC finally broke me, and I had no choice but to be listed actively. A MELD score and blood type are used to determine where an individual falls on the list. A patient with the worse conditions gets the preference. But the answer in these cases is to find a live donor that would be willing to donate a part of their liver. My youngest sister knew I was low on the donor list, volunteered to be tested to see if she was a match. Thankfully she was and the surgery was scheduled. Finally, I thought I had some hope.

I had surgery on December 9th, 2015, but very soon my body began to reject my sister's liver. In June of 2016 it was decided that I would have a trans jugular liver biopsy, where they go through the neck to reach the liver. I woke up from what should have been an outpatient procedure to complete hell. Something happened in the procedure, I had sepsis and other unknown infections. My body went into a complete shock, and I was hospitalized for close to a month, was put into a coma until my body could fight off all the infections that had occurred. Once again my liver had taken a major hit and I was became more ill.

In October of 2016 I was listed again for a transplant. This time frame is hard for me, and I have very few memories. When liver is not functioning, it causes hepatic encephalopathy. This feels like being extremely intoxicated and your state of mind is altered. But one thing I do remember is the doctors coming to my room and telling me that they have a liver for me. "Do you want it?" YES, absolutely I did. The surgery was set for the next day October 6th, 2016.

After my surgery I always wanted to know the person whose decision to be a donor had saved my life. I was given another chance at life to be a mom, a daughter, a sister, a friend, and a wife. Jim and I were married on June 11th, 2021. I had never imagined I would get a chance to be married and have such a beautiful wedding.

There are really no words to describe how thankful I am. Transplant gave me my life back.

I will forever be grateful for Rowi's decision to be a donor. There is not a day that goes by that I don't think of her. It has been an honor to get to know her family and learn what an amazing young woman she was. Her gift has extended my life and allowed me to enjoy five more years of many blessings.

Kristi is Rowi's lung recipient from Minnesota. We still haven't had the chance to meet her personally but hopefully soon we will. This is Kristi's story.

At age 22 I was diagnosed with pulmonary hypertension. I had my first transplant when I was 24. It wasn't until many years later that the function in those lungs started to deteriorate because of some type of antibody mediated rejection. May 15th, 2015, I was officially listed for new lungs again.

When I think back to what life was like before my transplant it seems unimaginable to admit how sick I really was. I'm somewhat of a perfectionist and it was hard to admit that I was declining and not going to bounce back and be normal. I kept waiting for my breathing to improve. But it didn't. It only continued to get worse. Much worse. Very reluctantly, I started wearing oxygen at night and eventually all day. The oxygen only helped so much, I was still struggling to breathe.

The hardest part of being sick was being a parent. Peyton was around the age of 5 when I was getting to my lowest point of health. My breathlessness interfered with everything. I couldn't run around with Peyton or take her to places I wanted to go with her. I couldn't do many of the fun things that kids do, like ride a bike, picking her up, getting stuff from the refrigerator, or even something as simple as blowing bubbles. I learned to be very calculated in order to conserve my breathing and keep my anxiety under control. I counted how many steps it would take me to get to different rooms with as few trips as possible, knowing that if I took too many steps I'd be left gasping for air. I had to keep Peyton on my bed at night, so I wouldn't have to walk all the way to her room. So, no matter where I went in our small hometown, the 50 feet of oxygen tubing accompanied me on that journey.

There were times when I thought about how life would be for Peyton if something happened to me. Peyton knew I was sick but didn't know to what extent. I myself didn't know if there was a possibility to find healthy lungs.

Amongst trying to maintain what little lung function I still had left, I had other things working against me like my weight dropping to the lower threshold for being eligible for transplant. I was below 85 pounds and antibodies that would not cooperate with new lungs. I had a lot of them in my system, which made the search for lungs much harder, leading to a 17 month wait on the transplant list.

On October 5th, 2016, while watching Peyton at gymnastics, I received an unexpected phone call. It was the moment of miracle and answered prayers that changed my life forever. It was the call for a healthy set of lungs. It was a whirlwind of emotions, happiness, relief, a true sense of joy but also great sadness and guilt knowing that a family was experiencing an irreplaceable loss at that very same moment.

In 2016, two families' lives changed forever. My life changed so dramatically. I recovered from surgery without any major events or setbacks. My doctors said I received the perfect set of lungs. After a couple of months living in Minneapolis near the hospital, I was finally able to move back home. Slowly my life was getting to normalcy. I was able to pick up Peyton from school, this time without the oxygen and losing my breath. I finished my pulmonary rehabilitation program and started gaining my strength back. A few months later I went back to work as a nurse, and also started school for my Master of Science in Nursing degree.

I also got married unknowingly on Rowena's birthday and have two great stepsons. We have been able to do so many wonderful things together that never would have been possible before. Driving the road to Hana on Maui, hiking up mountains and hot air ballooning in Sedona, watching sunrise and sunsets on the beaches of Florida. I enjoy and appreciate small things like every day walks, biking, attending kids events, hosting gatherings with family, and spoiling our two cats and bunnies. I feel like I was never sick and can accomplish anything I put my heart and mind to. I try to not take my easy breathing for granted.

I am forever grateful for the selfless gift I received from Rowena and her family. It is impossible to put into words how I feel. Going through something as significant as a transplant really puts things into perspective, you learn not to worry about the trivial things in life, but to cherish the important people and experiences you have.

Thank you Emily and Kristi for such kind and beautiful letters. We cannot wait to see Emily again and most certainly Kristi too. I want to put my hand and ears on Kristi's lungs and hear her breathe.

It's been nearly six years since Rowi's death but the grief hasn't lessened. No matter what anyone says the pain remains within me—within my entire family—and it will be there until that day when we join her in heaven.

People often say, "I understand your pain." But how can they when they haven't walked in our shoes? Empathy, yes, but true understanding, no. People also say, "Time will heal." But that doesn't happen either. It's still very much present. Grief hits me like a baseball bat out of nowhere, like a tsunami without warning.

Some people tell me that I am brave, to which I used to respond, "I didn't have a choice." Today, I believe I actually did have a choice. I could have become an alcoholic, a drug addict, or committed suicide but I didn't. I had to stay strong for my dad, B, and most importantly, Shad.

No matter what I was going through inside, the world seldom saw my pain. I'd smile, laugh, and joke because that's how I coped, and after Rowi's death, I knew that was what she'd want me to do.

Life has thrown me under the train more times than I can count. But I do remember these moments because they devastated my body, mind, and soul. Even with broken bones, a shattered heart, and fake smiles I managed to stand up again.

The time has come to not take a stand for me but to take one for others. I now see life through a different lens and realize how I had wasted so much time pleasing people or focusing on things that didn't matter or were not important. I am existing here and behind the face, I am a woman with pain, happiness, fond memories, and so many complicated emotions that sometimes I fear I'll forget to breathe. Just breathe.

EPILOGUE

For the longest time I couldn't help but focus on the question: why? Why had my life included so much suffering? Why was I being punished? Perhaps something from a past life. All these unanswered whys weighed on me so profoundly that they nearly paralyzed me. It led to me being nervous and bitter constantly—smoldering out the joy I was capable of giving and receiving too many times to mention.

After Rowi's passing, I couldn't help but blame myself. B and I went to countless grief sessions, but it made no difference. I was consumed by this grief.

Even though I wasn't ready to talk, my sweet cousin Danny who has grown into a fine caring motivational speaker didn't give up on me. After many hours of weekend conversations and struggles he tried convincing me to write just one word or sentence that I was grateful for. I failed; my grief and misery were way too much to think of anything to be grateful for, including Rowi's insistence that we take time off from life to do things together; especially her and Shad. She'd done that just two days before she was taken from this world, and we are so grateful to have listened. Perhaps it was our subconscious minds alerting us to treasure those moments.

One day, Dan made me realize something that I had never thought of before. Dan mentioned that things could have been worse, Rowi wasn't stabbed, burnt, tortured, raped, and thrown somewhere far away. She was in her own house surrounded by her two best friends.

What Dan said was absolutely true—and I was finally able to acknowledge the wisdom in his words. At first, they were received like a sharp knife to the gut. I finally picked up the pen and started with words I was grateful for and eventually words became sentences. After that I started writing letters to Rowi every single day. I knew these letters were not going to be mailed but somehow knew she would be reading them. Every single thing that I had wanted to tell her was in those daily letters. At times I couldn't write I drew pictures of whatever came in my mind's eye.

Slowly, I felt hope, which was something I'd been depriving myself of for a long time. This process didn't happen within a day or so, it took me a few months to feel the peace coming in. I started meditating, did regular yoga and Tai- chi classes, reiki sessions, and relied on the help of an empath to explore my connection to Rowi in her new world. However, what I found to be most transformational for my inner peace was being able to help others in need.

I'm not rich so it wasn't necessarily with money; it has been a warm hug, good listening ears, or a hot mug of fresh coffee with a muffin for a homeless person. These magical moments of giving a smile to someone else have helped me in the most brilliant ways. My only condition: I don't have any strings attached. I just give because it feels right, and I know my angel is smiling at me from above.

In 2019, Melesa Coffey, a wonderful parent at Wichita Montessori School, suggested to start a scholarship for Psychology at Wichita State University in Rowena's name. It was a beautiful thought but I had to ask: where do I get that kind of money?

Melesa introduced me to Aaron Winter, Director of Development, and Amy Tully, Associate Director of Development. Our very first meeting with them was on January 11, 2019, at Starbucks.

We had several meetings before Shad made a video talking about Rowi's tragic death and requesting for scholarship funds. It was absolutely unbelievable but within ten days we had $10,000 in a WSU scholarship account. It didn't end there; the donations kept coming and we reached our goal of $40,000 for the endowment. B, Shad, and I were so dumb struck and humbled for all the wonderful donors.

Up to this point, nine psychology students have been awarded $500 each. We have met three of these students personally. Though $500 is not a huge amount of money where college expenses are concerned, these students are working toward amazing ways to contribute to the world. It has provided us with a sense of peace and another connection to Rowi. We hope and pray to grow the Rowena Irani Psychology Endowment so more students can benefit. My Rowena's name will live on forever and no one can take that away from me. NO ONE!

My dear reader, if there is one thing that you should take away from my sorrow and the circumstances I have been forced to face, it is that you should cherish every day and moment for the people you can impact, whether they are family, friends, or strangers.

* * *

July 2021, B, Shad, and I moved away from Kansas. We left Wichita, our forever friends, and our home to start a new life. The memories will always exist, the pain will always be fought, but the fresh start helps us find the tenacity to go another day.

Life is ever-unpredictable. Live your life to its fullest and view each day as a true blessing, as tomorrow is not promised. When you find those coins in your car unexpectedly, use them to be reminded of some of the best moments of your life.

For image gallery, American Monster documentary, and more, please scan the code below or visit www.ToranjIrani.com.

SCAN ME